The Rise and Fall of the British Manager

Alistair Mant is a famous iconoclast of the 'management' field, which he sees as a form of fairyland. He was born in Australia and read history at the University of Sydney, after which he went into the advertising business. Subsequently he began a long association with the IBM Corporation, most of it in the management development field. 'When I first applied to IBM,' he admits, 'I had no idea what the letters stood for and when I first accepted an appointment in management development I didn't know what that was either. I still don't.'

He has a distinguished career in education, consultancy and research and wrote the celebrated *Mant Report* on the development of managerial people in mid-career. For this work he was awarded the British Institute of Management's Bowie Medal in 1972. As a businessman he achieved some notoriety as the inventor and exploiter of the world's first double-sided nude jigsaw puzzle, a successful combination of a novelty product and management education project.

He has had a long association with the Tavistock Institute in London in both educational and research work and is a regular broadcaster, lecturer and contributor to journals. He works as consultant to a wide range of industrial and non-industrial organizations. He lives in London with his wife and two daughters and his consuming passion, outside family and work, is music.

'Alistair Mant is an Australian – among the most original, it is now apparent, of his generation – and he seems to have come up with an analysis of this country's present condition which nobody else has quite matched for depth and point.' *New Statesman*

D1092609

Alistair Mant

The Rise and Fall
of the British Manager

revised edition

illustrations by the author

Pan Books
in association with The Macmillan Press

First published 1977 by The Macmillan Press Ltd
This revised edition published 1979 by Pan Books Ltd,
Cavaye Place, London SW10 9PG
© Alistair Mant 1977, 1979
ISBN 0 330 25703 X
Printed and bound in Great Britain by
Hazell Watson & Viney Ltd, Aylesbury, Bucks

Contents

Preface 7

Introduction: Management – what does it mean? 11

1 The linguistics of management 15

2 The rise of the British manager 31

3 A culture of dependence 59

4 The post-war managers 86

5 A word for the product 95

6 Management development – a new priesthood 121

7 The informal world of management development 134

8 Management education 159

9 The case for a national neurosis 172

10 Fighting the good fight 181

Conclusion 207

Bibliography 209

Index 213

Preface

This is not a book which elicits moderate responses. You either love it, or you hate it, if the critics' response to the first edition is any guide. It was written in rather a hurry and with feeling, for therapy. In the summer of 1976, I was stuck in the writing of another, more scholarly, work. At that time, certain inappropriate ideas and phrases kept appearing on the page in front of me, until it became clear that there was a different book in the system, demanding to be let out. This is it, somewhat modified; and therapeutic it was to release it to the four winds.

This is not an uncommon experience for writers, especially in the case of non-fiction writers, in their late thirties (i.e., mid-life). There is, it seems, a need to pull threads together and get them out of the guts on to paper, before moving on to new work. It happens that, as I was struggling with all this, I re-read Liam Hudson's marvellous dissection of the world of psychological research, *The Cult of the Fact*, just to check a reference. In the opening chapter, he recounts exactly the same experience and he was, at the time of writing it (or at the time it popped out) about the same age.

In re-working this edition, I have resisted the temptation to make the book less irritating – otherwise it would be a different book. In particular, I have largely ignored suggestions that it ought to be more 'constructive' – that it 'ought' to make recommendations about what 'ought' to happen in the world of management. I have done this for two reasons. Firstly, I irritated the right people, it seems to me, last time round; and, secondly, I don't believe many people are really in the dark about some of the straightforward, low-key, but daunting decisions staring us all in the face. People may be fearful, but they are not clueless.

In addition, the nature of the original book, for all its many flaws, had the character of a management act – discharged quickly, under pressure, with a *survival* element present. Managers at work understand this and seem to respond to it; sometimes it is more important to get something *done*, than to get it exactly right. Anyway, the writing of a book is an impotent act, if no one, or hardly anyone, reads the product or is affected by it. By that criterion, ninety-nine per cent of 'management' books are celebrations of impotence – and thus, essentially, unmanagerial.

Most of the managers I know never read books at all. Very few seriously challenge their ideas about their work and the efficacy of their work roles. Very many are unaware that they *have* deep-rooted ideas about such things which govern their actions or, more likely, inactions at work. If I succeed in making a manager *think* about all this, even if it is an unscientific, irreverent or a silly thought, we may have made some progress.

It isn't easy to prepare the reader for the contents herein. There are four main threads:

1 Historical Chapters 2 and 4 trace the emergence of a 'management' movement in the first place and the conscious and unconscious ideas of a 'manager' that went with it. This is not meant to be serious scholastic history but simply an indication that important things change slowly, usually by evolutionary processes, and we inherit many of our ideas about them.

2 Linguistic Chapter 1 in particular deals with the linguistic imprecision and obfuscation of management-speak, though it is a recurrent theme throughout the book. As the English language gave the world 'management', the language itself must be part of the study of the subject.

3 Social-anthropological A grand way of saying that the concept of 'management' is culture-bound and, in order to understand it, we have to study the particular culture that gave rise to it. Chapter 3 contrasts the Dependent cultural assumptions of Britain with the Fight-oriented assumptions of America and other more industrially successful countries.

4 Experiential/anecdotal I have spent most of my working life in industry and, in that time, a great many strange and awful things have happened to me. Accounts of these are dotted about the book here and there.

There is little new in any of this, and I am certainly an amateur in history, linguistics and social science, but I have not found this particular *combination* anywhere else. It may therefore be helpful for those at, or near, my own point of departure. Despite the parochial title, the book is for *all* English-speaking managers – Americans (for whom I have worked, in the IBM Corporation, for years), – Australians (with whom, being one myself, I grew up) and others.

In a way, the heart, or engine-room, of the book is Chapter 5. This is an attempt to recall that Authority comes not from the clouds but arises from Work and Outputs. There is nothing new here either, but we are in an odd situation when such things still need to be said. Later chapters (6 to 8) deal with managerial careers and education and their connection, if any, with Work. This may be of particular interest to specialist readers, though the issues bear on all careers, in and outside 'industry'. Finally, in Chapters 9 to 10, I muse on Britain as the forerunner into post-industrial society. This is a popular sport these days and, as I am neither blandly optimistic *nor* plunged in gloom about the topic, the musings may fill a useful gap in the middle-ground.

I owe many people many debts in relation to the book, though none of them can be blamed for it. My time at the Tavistock Institute in London (and latterly my association with the Grubb Institute of Behavioural Studies) has been invaluable. In particular, the ideas of Dr W. R. Bion, the late Dr A. K. Rice, Dr Eric Miller, and Bruce Reed, have influenced my thinking on the psychological aspects of culture. Professor John Morris (of the Manchester Business School) and Professor Reg Revans taught me much of what I know about the education of managers and John Morris helped me to see how funny a lot of it was. More recently, Lord Wilfred Brown has made me think very hard about the institutional, as opposed to behavioural, side of management activity.

I owe a debt also to the Social Science Research Council of Great Britain for support in research into management careers and management education. Geoff Bell contributed research assistance for the book, Rita Friend typed the original manuscript with superb attention to detail, and my wife and daughters – an ill-managed group at the best of times – have put up with a great deal as the book has ground its way to this edition.

AM, London 1979

Introduction:
Management – what does it mean?

The idea for this book came originally from two apparently quite different experiences. One was connected with the experience of getting married and having children. In those days I was styled a 'manager' and my wife, so far as the tax people were concerned, was a 'housewife'. I can remember well the blessed relief of leaving my house and its attendant chaos each morning to go off to my oh-so-demanding 'management' job. In what sense, I had to ask myself in the end, was my wife not 'managing' and in what sense was my work more difficult or more essentially *managerial* than hers? At work, I had another woman to make sure I managed properly. This one was paid, indeed positively relied on, to nag me about detail in precisely the way that my wife was (and is) not allowed to. This one wasn't styled a 'manager' either, but the same essential question held good for her; in what sense is the work of a secretary *not* managerial?

By this time, I was beginning to be worried about the meaning of 'management' and 'manager' – if they meant anything at all. There was, of course, a largish industry, to which I belonged, in management literature, management education, management development and all the rest of it, but, what was it all about? Could all those people – the pundits, the professors, the managers themselves – be on about nothing or, more likely, could they be on about so many things that it made no sense at all to lump them together under the banner 'management'.

The other experience led me in exactly the same direction. I found myself asked by a senior sales manager of a big American firm to examine a department that was, in his estimation, not 'professional' enough in its performance. My ears pricked up at the mention of the word 'professional' because it happens to be another of those words that often seems to mean nothing at all, or so much that one word won't do. So far as he was concerned, this department, a 'marketing support' department, had objectives handed down from above that were not being achieved and so, he assumed, the logical thing to do was to attempt to narrow the gap between aspiration and performance.

The first, and fundamental, discovery about this 'unprofessional' group of men was that no one, save the manager, had been there longer than two years and, what's more, such had always been the case. Without continuity, there was no way, in my view, that 'professional' levels of performance could be achieved when the task was to supply quite complex information to the field about products, prices, specifications and so on. Before we tried to change the performance level, it seemed to make sense to ask why a biggish sub-system of a major firm could so delude itself about its situation for so long. The answer, in hindsight, was fairly simple; salesmen get tired – they have a lousy job, largely devoid of legitimacy in the eyes of society and they live on their nerves. Rejection of the product by the customer feels like personal rejection because the salesman, to a large extent, uses himself to sell it. Much as he would like to, he can't linger too long with his favourite clients – not if he wants to make any money that week.

No wonder then that salesmen will frequently do anything to get into 'management' – into work which society deems clean rather than dirty and where you can actually compel people to do things for a change. Most of the salesmen I know tend to be in debt up to their eyeballs, but they still seem to be prepared to accept a substantial drop in earnings in order to enter the magic brotherhood of 'management'. If only you could promote all the salesmen into management everything would be fine – until you went broke, of course.

Which brings us back to 'marketing support' and its true function in life, namely, casualty clearing station for shell-shocked salesmen – a place to go for a couple of years under the guise of 'broadening' or some other euphemism, but with no commitment to promotion. Why not just call it a casualty clearing station? – that would mean facing up to what the sales life does to people and, for that matter, to their marriages. Most commercial firms haven't arrived at that point yet.

The story has two morals. One, it is apparently worth making a lot of sacrifices to retreat from the field into a tiny office or cubicle with 'manager' on the door. Two, there is a paradox in the manager-salesman relationship; the salesman's job is shot through with technical skill, leadership and trusteeship – *he* goes into the environment and, so to speak, takes the skin of the organization with him when he goes; – he *is* the organization so far as his prospects and clients experience it. His implicit authority is almost boundless; all he is really accountable for is to bring home the bacon. How he does it is up to him.

His 'manager', on the other hand, occupies the archetypal 'Mickey Mouse' job. He has to control the salesmen's creative energies so that the market place is made to adapt to last month's production schedules, rather than vice versa. He has to tot up the figures and pass them on for higher-order collation like any postboy; and, he is supposed to 'motivate' the salesmen – that is, to try to cause grown men to become excited over some bauble put up as the monthly sales-contest prize. If a salesman has something important on his mind, he will probably go at least two up the line to talk about it, leap-frogging the interposing 'Mickey Mouse', in search of a mature dependency figure.

Of course, it depends how you define management but, to all intents and purposes, it seemed to me that the salesmen, for all their frailties, did a great deal of 'managing' and the first-line manager hardly any at all. Taken together, these anecdotes seem to me to have some pungency. In a country like Britain, patently unable to compete successfully in international trade and rapidly approaching collective poverty, the jobs of salesmen and housewife seem to take on a special importance. The one, because it creates wealth directly and the other because it provides the glue to hold together communities in danger of falling apart and does so cheaper and more humanely than the local social services manager.

Yet, for many people, the burden for putting things right seems to rest primarily on the shoulders of the 'managers' – that is, those people who have managed to put details behind them in order to concentrate on the 'broad picture'. I don't have anything against the broad picture, but I know that the only really successful managers I have met manage to do *both* – to keep an eye on the big things that count while paying meticulous attention to the little things that count as well. There is not a lot of point in understanding child psychology backwards if you don't attend to (say) dirty nappies, or cut knees, at precisely the time the fates decree that you must. Any *production* manager worth his salt understands this – i.e. that the operation of a factory calls for the same, almost feminine, capacity to sense that something horrible is about to happen, just before it does. It is not a sense, or instinct, that is kept alive by that total absorption in the broad picture that many managers seem to think represents their role in life. This provides us with a further irony of the scene – the low status of production in Britain, vis-à-vis other specialisms, in a country desperately in need of products that halfway sell themselves on quality alone.

The puzzle, then, is to understand why we downgrade so many of the jobs that really matter whilst building around the idea of 'management' a plethora of myths, shibboleths and incantations which our most successful competitors seem to be able to do without. When I sat down to write this, I had in mind the thousands of young men and (more so, now) women who will be taking on the role of 'manager' in the future. What on earth will they make of it and how can they be helped to understand that, if 'management' doesn't mean running things properly (no excuses) then it doesn't really mean anything at all?

1 The linguistics of management

Managers often say to me, when I start to get pernickety about the words we use – 'That's just a matter of semantics!' Words may indeed be blunt instruments, but they are the only instruments we have got if we want to understand each other. I may, or may not, have in my head the same idea as you but, until somebody finds a way of plugging directly into your cortical circuitry, I have to use words to find out, and so do you. If it turns out that we assign different meanings to the same words, we are stuck and, worse still, we have to use even more words to check if it is so.

Britain, for her sins, gave the world 'management' and so, if we want to understand the word in all its many meanings, we have to attend to the English language itself. It is a better language than any other for drama, richness of description and poetry (from Shakespeare to dirty limericks) but it is also the best language for obfuscation, evasion and gobbledegook. Americans, Canadians, Australians and the other colonials are stuck with it and, in business culture, an increasing number of others are having to come to terms with it too.

It always surprises me how little English-speakers are aware that 'management', seen as a professional specialism, is a product of Anglo-Saxon culture. It is as if, girdling the globe, a brotherhood of 'managers' can be found, united in ideals, purpose and mode of operation. Equally, I am always surprised how little attention is paid to the Germans, whose ideas about running things tend to be different and, more important, whose industrial performance, for seventy years at least, has been quite different. The cynical may even posit a direct correlation between the amount of money spent on management education and development in Britain and the rate of decline in industrial performance. In Germany, they have traditionally had no management education at all, as such, and have apparently not needed it. Why? How can you run such successful enterprises without any 'management'?

Of course, they have management, in the sense of running things, but they have done without a management movement and a specialized management language and this tells us something very important about them and us. When we talk of the 'profession of management', this would be doubly meaningless in Germany because neither is there a word for 'professional' in the loaded sense we use it. Yet, if we judge an industry's professionalism by the integrity of its end products, the Germans are professional by anybody's standards. Note the plaintive observations of a group of managers from the North-West Middlesex branch of the British Institute of Management on a visit to Dusseldorf, reported in March 1976:

Manager identification In trying to define the role of the manager, the group experienced difficulty in identifying who in an organization could be regarded as a manager. In the end a negative definition was accepted because certain grades of staff workers and supervisors are not eligible for election to the Works Council, the organ of German industrial democracy common to virtually all businesses. Thus, a manager was defined as an employee who was designated to enter into contract, to sign cheques or to engage and dismiss subordinates. Quite senior employees – and in Germany employees represent a privileged group enjoying 'staff' status – with some management responsibilities are eligible for election to the Works Council and would in the United Kingdom possibly belong to one of the several management institutes.

Professional management institutes The word 'professional', in any discussion with German managers, generally proved to be an obstacle to the understanding of the role of manager. A notable exception was the D.G.F.P. (German Society for Personnel Management) whose Director possessed both a command of the English language and an understanding of the function of the professional body in British society.

Many managers were highly educated in specialist subjects to the level of doctorate and for this group any training for management had to be practical after what, by British standards, would be regarded as an excessive period of higher education lasting until the age of 30 or beyond. 'Management education' not surprisingly, had no German equivalent.

And finally – the manager as a third force. Since it was not easy to identify the manager, the group found difficulty in securing any agreement among the organizations visited on the issue of the special role of the manager in society.

Comment is almost superfluous; if only more English-language managers could suffer similar culture-shock and reflect on it, our management language might begin to make more sense.

These complications amount to more than simply a series of linguistic quirks. The fact that in the English language we have nurtured the idea of management – an idea which, as I suggested above, largely resists clarification – *means* something. It looks, in fact, suspiciously like what the Americans call a 'motherhood' concept, like 'democracy', 'participation' and other such words. A motherhood concept is one about which people feel approving and which they wish to preserve in a good, idealized state. More often than not, the best way to do this is to keep the idea as vague as possible so that it can never be inspected minutely or knocked down. This is my experience of the idea of management in Britain – that is, that large numbers of highly-paid, otherwise intelligent people are prepared to think about it, talk about it and write about it without ever checking what the other fellow means by it. Indeed, I have got so far as this chapter without spelling out what *I* mean by it. Not for long.

The clue to this odd use of language may be found in traditional British approaches to 'science'. Nowhere in Continental Europe does one find the extraordinary English-language split of 'pure' and 'applied' science. In Britain, the arts are definitely OK, 'pure' science is *quite* OK (but not so OK as the arts) and 'applied' science is definitely the fag-end of the classificatory system. It is difficult to interpret such a classification without imagining that applied science really represents a euphemistic way of saying manufacturing, but it sounds a bit better – more 'scientific'. The truth is that, so far as research can establish, 'pure' science is hardly ever the source of commercial advance. The breakthroughs tend to come from intelligent and hard-working attempts to improve the performance of existing products, rather than the application of new scientific knowledge. 'In truth, possession of scientific know-ledge simply does not transmit easily into economic and industrial strength. The emperor with all the Nobel Prize winners he wants, but who has neglected the arts of *Technik*, will be found out to be naked as the day he was born.' Indeed, 'those with Nobel Prizes in physics or biology are much less likely to be heeded on topics of manufacturing in Germany than in Britain.' (Fores, M., unpublished paper.)

If we examine the equivalent Continental words, in so far as they exist, we find, for example, *Kunst* (the fine arts), *Wissen-schaft* (the broader conception of science as a way of approach-ing all phenomena methodically in order to understand them) and, finally, *Technik* (manufacture). The point of this classi-fication is that it does *not* fudge the boundary between the arts and science, nor the boundary between science and manu-facture. In Germany, a historian, as an analyst of data, is not regarded as part of the arts and an engineer is astounded to find his English counterparts described as 'scientists'. Most important of all, manufacture has a separate and valued iden-tity, its own educational system, its own cultural shrines. Because of this, those engaged in manufacturing have no real need to pretend to be anything they are not.

What the use of language tells us is that the British, and especially the 'opinion formers', try to fit concepts of this sort into a kind of over-simple binary coding system, what I call British Binary Thought.

The net result is to split important areas of endeavour and thought into (effectively) clean and dirty compartments. Thus, while applied science has to mean machines, grime, oily rags, soot, effluent, etc., 'pure' is the word most preferred by the soap manufacturers, almost as though soap were not the end product of a manufacturing process. What the language denies is the substantial *middle ground* where, in an integrated system, or, for that matter, within a human being with integrity, the opposites overlap. It will be noted that, in such a binary mode of classification, the same person may appear on either side of the respectability line, depending on the viewer. It is non-U to work in industry, but, if you must, it has its (relatively) respectable side. In New York, you ought to be a WASP, but if you happen to be a black, there is always the Puerto Ricans (or vice versa).

Clean	Dirty
U	Non-U
Effortless	Hard Working
Pure Science	Applied Science
The professions	Industry
Gentle-men	Hard Men
Brains	Hands
Generalist	Specialist
But:	
Management	Workers
and:	
Eye Specialist	Gynaecologist

Likewise, the inclusion of eye specialist and gynaecologist in the list requires explanation. One of the few genuinely funny bits of research in recent years was Liam Hudson's correlation of the social origin of British doctors with the parts of the body on which they later specialized. What he discovered was a statistically valid correlation between social background and U and non-U specialisms. Those from English public schools showed a significant tendency to specialize in work on the head as opposed to the body below the waist, the surface of the body as opposed to its innards, the living body as opposed to the dead body and the male body as opposed to the female body. This fact bore little relationship to professional status – it goes deeper than that; into subconscious perceptions of cleanliness and dirtiness. (Clearly, the boardroom is the head and the factory the bowels of British industry.) Of course, all doctors belong on the clean side, vis-à-vis industry, but some are cleaner than others; they have their own aristocracy.

The real point of this sort of comparison is that 'management' is now, on the whole, clean. It was not always so. The word 'manage' derives from two quite distinct sources. The first is the Italian word *maneggiare* which (roughly translated) meant handling things (Latin *manus*, a hand) and especially horses. In this derivation it was ultimately a masculine concept, to do with taking charge, directing, especially in the context of war. The word 'manage' carried this broader sense by the beginning of the sixteenth century, but soon it became confused with the French *menager*, which meant careful use (especially in a

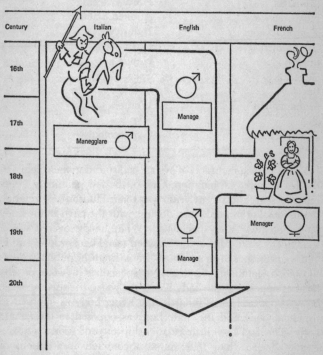

The meanings of management (1) The underlying derivation of English-language 'management' – i.e. the hermaphrodite outcome of the fusion of masculine and feminine conceptions borrowed from other cultures (*maneggiare* – the handling of horses and men in war and *menager* – careful housekeeping)

household) or a careful housekeeper – altogether a more gentle, perhaps feminine, usage. The idea of management seems to have kept this dual character ever since. We use it to describe a technical activity, usually in relation to 'industry' and also in relation to the handling of men (standing in for horses) but we also use it as a synonym for simply coping in any kind of situation. Thus the 'professional manager' may, at the end of the day, ask the wife with two sick children to cope with – 'Did you manage all right?' Managing therefore refers to the handling of technical processes as well as the handling of people. Sometimes it is then wrapped up as 'personnel management' – 'the more negotiable, because more abstract, phrase is "personnel management", where the human beings on each side of the process (i.e. bosses and workers) have been fully generalized and abstracted.' (Raymond Williams, *Keywords*.)

The first 'managers' were really no more than agents of owners or those in charge of public institutions such as workhouses. The operative change in the nineteenth century was probably the steady increase in the *size* of organizations so that, beginning with one or two agents, it made sense in time to talk about 'the management', that is, a body of people acting for the owners. At this point, the concept of 'manager' was a neutral one, even pejorative. Thus, Robert Owen, writing in 1811: 'My intention was not to be a *mere* manager'. 'We rely not upon management *or trickery*, but upon our own hearts and hands' (Jowett, 1881). 'Talent for *intrigue or management* usually counts for more than debating power' (Bryce, 1888). In the

---

The meanings of management (2); the manager as not a worker. The transmutation of 'management' from a neutral verb of action (doing) to a respectable state of *being*, occurred in the nineteenth century. From that point, in Anglo-Saxon culture, management no longer meant simply another type of worker, but *not* a worker at all; thus:

DIRTY	CLEAN

"Worker"   *vs*   "Manager"

more refined employments – the colonial and civil services – there were no managers but 'administrators'.

America must take the credit, if that is the right word, for beginning the process of pumping 'management' full of legitimation and, although the great 'scientific' managerial thinkers were writing at a time of great industrial turmoil, the Americans had no hangover from the industrial revolution on the scale of Britain – in the land of opportunity anyone might succeed according to his lights, to the greater glory of self, country and God. The origins of this attitude may be seen in the writings of Taylor, the doyen of management theorists. As Bendix comments, 'Taylor took the concept of management away from the traditional employers and agents. Management's task became to get the best out of men, for benefit of all – but this required chiefly the application of scientific methods by managers . . . From a man whose success in the world made him a natural leader, the manager became a leader of men whose success depended in part upon a science which would place each man "in the highest class of work for which his natural abilities fit him" [Taylor] . . . the manager or executive was being transformed from a person whose success made his superiority self-evident into one whose success was due to managerial abilities which required analysis and specialized training.'

By the 1960s, the American vision of the manager could be expressed in, so far as I am aware, a perfectly serious book (C. S. George Jnr, *The History of Management Thought*).

Management is the determiner of our economic *progress*, the employer of our educated, the amasser of our resources, the *strength* of our *national defense*, and the *moulder* of our *society*. It is the *core* of all our *public* as well as *personal* activities . . . as we know it today, it is, in some respects, a twentieth-century concept. It has attained its position however through the efforts of a host of men working on its behalf over the centuries. It *stands tall* because it stands on the shoulders of past theoreticians and scholars – a *meaningful product of history* . . . today's manager recognises his multiple *obligations* because of his peculiar place of *stewardship* over vast resources. The employees' and *community's well-being* takes equal or greater precedence over owners and customers in many matters.

Borrowing from all schools of managerial thought, today's manager is eclectic in his practice. In fact, we might call his new brand of management a somewhat *scientifically humanized approach* – one incorporating all the findings of the sociologist and psychologist, yet still managing to be quantitatively oriented (sic) with a goodly portion of *scientific methodology*. Imbued with the idea of research, today's manager is *open-minded* in virtually all spheres, standing *ready to promote change* if his *science* shows it to be more effective.

Count the motherhood words and phrases; from Owen's 'mere manager' we have come, finally, to supermanager.

This is not the first, nor will it be the last, example of Americans doing strange and wonderful things with the English language. If Queen Elizabeth I could call booty 'curiosities', why should not the Americans describe bribery as 'influence expenditure'. The case of management is not dissimilar. Reddin, one of the more eminent of the North American management gurus, insists that 'management' is a culture-free concept. What's more, he appears to believe it; to the Americans perhaps it *is* culture-free – a pure expression of the virtues of hard work, application of practical intelligence and fair dealing. The tragedy is that the British have reimported so many words from the Americas, believing them still to mean roughly the same as they did on export. Management is such a word. 'Scientific' management in America actually meant using analytic means to find more efficient ways of running enterprises and, possibly, keeping labour quiet. The lure of 'scientific' management in Britain was that it clutched the coat-tails of 'science' and thus may have helped to disguise what we all suspect – that business is really a dirty game.

The use of the word management in America has always been a Germanic, Lutheran use – just as the language of management as a whole has assumed the ponderous, building-on structure of German language and thought. It is not commonly known to Englishmen that the Continental Congress of the USA once voted on whether German or English ought to be the official language of America. German lost, by very few votes, and that narrow squeak may have done more to confuse the issues in *British* management than any other event

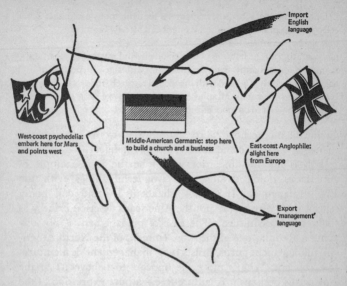

West-coast psychedelia: embark here for Mars and points west

Middle-American Germanic: stop here to build a church and a business

East-coast Anglophile: alight here from Europe

Import English language

Export 'management' language

before or since. Since then we have observed a stream of Germanic management ideas, dressed up in a kind of English, re-entering British industrial and business culture and re-entering it, as often as not, in the form of holy writ. Much of it has in fact been incomprehensible in British culture but this has dimmed hardly anybody's enthusiasm. Look at this example of mid-Atlantic management-speak – the official (BIM 1966) attempt at a definitive statement about the management activity: 'Responsibility for judgement of the decision in effectively planning, motivating and controlling operations towards known objectives attained through efficient cooperation of the personnel concerned.' It certainly isn't English and, to be fair, it must have been larded together by a committee; nonetheless, it demonstrates the linguistic muddle to near perfection.

The British colonies inherit these same problems in an even more complicated form. In Australia, for example, there is 'management' but it is a weird amalgam of differing British and American conceptions about task and authority. Australia and Australian organizations look, to the superficial observer, rather American; under the skin they are irredeemably British, though not proud of it. Denial of this reality simply confuses the 'management' issue further; makes it more difficult for a distinctive Australian approach to running things properly (my construction of 'management') to emerge. Instead, there is a strange mix of Irish-Italian union power ranged against a complex Establishment of absentee leaders, increasingly infiltrated by the new Middle-Europeans. I have always said, and only half in joking, that the Hungarians are bound to take over the mainstream of Australian commercial life precisely because they spend rather less time than their competitors drinking, gambling, lying in the sun and otherwise wallowing in hedonism. Of course, by that time, they will be no longer Hungarians, any more than the Duponts, Rockefellers and Vanderbilts are French, Dutch or whatever.

The prestigious Jackson Committee on Australian Manufacturing Industry spelled out much that was wrong, or just plain sleepy, in Australian management in facing up to the changing ground-rules for wider participation in organizational decision-making: 'Australian managers generally are ill-prepared for these responsibilities and pressures.' The Jackson Committee called for a 'general debate on the shop floor, in management offices and in union offices'. Australia is still waiting for that debate. On a recent visit, an old boss of mine put it succinctly: 'If we can't blame the Government for everything, we blame the media; if that doesn't work, we blame émigré British shop stewards. By the way, we think OPEC is a Hungarian pianist!' (See Chapter 3 on Cultures of Dependence.) The best of all three cultures, British, American and middle-European, would represent a valuable new conception of management. The risk is that Australian management will fall between stools – wanting to shrug off the Raj, but suspicious of US economic domination and falling, all the while, under the sway of the remoter middle-European immigrants.

So, after all, 'management', from origins in a rather agreeable, Romance (Franco-Italian) concept, essentially practical (describing homely activities) and hermaphrodite as well, found the Germans moving in (via America) with a charge of Wagnerian philosophy so that the poor word was never the same again – overblown, fulsome and flatulent. As John Child has rightly pointed out, since the beginning of the twentieth century the word has to be seen in at least two different lights – firstly a description of activities and, secondly, an expression of a value or a collection of values. At the same time, with the steady increase in the size of organizations, it also, inevitably, came to mean a body of people associated with those activities and values – the managers.

Before I leave linguistics, there are two other words which bear close looking at: 'industry' and 'career'. The most straightforward definition of the word 'industry' derives from the convention adopted by statisticians. Thus 'industrial production' refers to all the output of a manufacturing sector, plus some of the output of public utilities, such as electricity generation. 'Industry' and 'manufacturing industry' are therefore different, but not much so.

What then are we up to in talking about a fishing industry, an agricultural industry, or the insurance industry? What does the Hospital Employees Union representative mean when he says – 'This will never happen in our industry'? The answer appears to be that industry, used thus, fits the split picture of society as divided into two parts, one clean and the other dirty. In British mythology, there is thought to have been a time when everybody was free and every aspect pleased: woodsmoke wisped from thatched cottages, the sun shone, yokels rumbled on about the seasons and God was in his Heaven. Then (according to the myth) there was the Industrial Revolution, smoke now belched in acrid plumes from tall and grimy stacks, men were everywhere in chains and a darkness fell upon the land. Something had gone wrong and, in the way of social systems, someone or something had to bear the burden of it. From that day to this, everybody's hang-ups about conflict, rigour and the harsh realities of life have been projected, usually unconsciously, on to 'industry' – whatever that is. (If the British fantasy is that some time, somewhere, freedom was lost, the American fantasy is that since 1776, or there-abouts, it has been secured.)

The truth is, there never was a time when Englishmen were free; and the 'Industrial Revolution' was, for the most part, neither a revolution, nor particularly industrial.

In the history books we read that the period of the first British Industrial Revolution was bound up with cotton, with the invention and use of new machinery, and with steam power. Certainly there were changes at this time. Water, and then steam, were used to power machinery in factories; the 'putting out' system in textile manufacture, with operatives working at home, was changed in favour of bringing most processes under a single roof. Some significant inventions were made, but the principal changes of the time are ill-described by the phrase 'Industrial Revolution'. A few facts show this clearly.

To start with cotton was never as important as many studies imply; there were more people employed in domestic service throughout the whole of the period 1760 to 1900. Even by 1801 the West Riding of Yorkshire, one of the main new areas for manufacturing, could be described as 'a country of industrialized villages'. Water power was more important than steam power for manufacturing right up to the end of the 'revolutionary' period. There were more employees in agriculture than in manufacturing up until 1815. There was no marked 'take off' from lower to higher levels of investment.

Charles Dickens' stories of young children being maltreated in a new era were mainly concentrated on schools, shops and workhouses. Charles Kingsley's 'Water Babies' were chimney sweeps, hardly parts of a new 'industrial' heritage in Britain. Manufacturing does not figure exclusively, or even extensively, as a harsh employer of the times; the mines and domestic service were probably worse. Factories and cotton may have been two *symbols* of the first half of the 19th century, but so were the public schools, the canals, and the new importance of Manchester primarily as a centre for commerce rather than for manufacturing. (Fores and Lawrence.)

My guess is that what the British really abhor is *cities*, or indeed any *too-large* concentration of people, as they sense it. It is what gives the country its peculiar grace and charm. Somehow the Industrial Revolution became the scapegoat for a much-too-fast process of urbanization. A Swedish manager won't let you out of the factory until you have seen the latest gadget they are cooking up to beat the Germans (or whomever) in some market or other. The British manager won't let you escape till he has established his rural or semi-rural bona fides; he may *work* in industry, but he jolly well *lives*, or retreats at weekends, to a determinedly rustic existence, surrounded (as one put it to me, with *pride*) by 'professional types'. The Swede goes rustic at weekends too, but to enjoy the outdoors for its own sake and not with the same sense of distaste for what is left behind.

As to 'industrial relations', I am in the habit of pointing out to clients that it is not so much a question of having 'good' or 'bad' industrial relations; once you have industrial relations at all, you are probably sunk. If you hire an industrial relations expert, he will have been schooled in the history of the Industrial Revolution and taught to define trouble of almost any kind as 'industrial relations', or vice versa, and, seeing the world in that light, it won't be long before you have lots and lots of 'industrial relations'. It probably won't be long before you are broke either.

On page 83 I detail my experience with Swedish firms in Britain. 'Industrial relations' doesn't really mean very much to the Swedes, which is their salvation. But in Sweden you are likely to find a factory, rather than fairies, at the bottom of your garden, no matter how respectable your suburb. Indeed, Renault is in Paris, Siemens in Berlin, Electrolux in Stockholm, Ford in Cologne, Hoechst in Frankfurt, SKF in Göteborg, and American industry all over America in small concentrations, notwithstanding the great centres. Only in Britain does one find that great swathe of service-sector employment, and respectability, clustered round London and the Home Counties. 'Industry' has been shoved up north, like the grisly corpse tucked up a chimney by the ape in the Rue Morgue.

'Industry' is 'out there' somewhere (up there on the map) and everything about it spells trouble. 'Industrial action' means strikes, 'industrial employment' means soul-less jobs, 'industrial establishments' means satanic mills, public housing for industrial workers means slums. The word 'industry' is therefore a receptacle for everything that is down-market, tasteless and lumpen. Oddly, those who sit in relative comfort in the south-east take a perverse pride in the Industrial Revolution, like Concorde, as a British first.

The last word I want to inspect is 'career' in the context of a 'career in management'. It is only in very recent times (that is, this century) that 'career' took on the sense of an orderly progress through a 'career structure'. The 'career development' officer is an even newer and stranger phenomenon. Previously, careering or 'careering about' meant galloping along in an unrestrained way, like somebody ricocheting off the walls of a squash-court.

The point is that for the vast majority of people *work* does not necessarily mean a career, it means *work* (more or less satisfying in itself), money and survival. But to go into 'management' is to join a club with, it is supposed, known and orderly rules and the hope of 'career advancement' ahead. You may do more or less well in the career, but it isn't exactly a question of survival, or at least it wasn't before the world-wide economic downturn began to bite. To take up a 'career in industrial management' means, therefore, to join a club (career) in an insalubrious area (industry) with the vaguest of constitutions and purposes (management).

It is here that the language reflects the awful split in British education between state and private schooling. Those who go into 'management' (not excluding management education, management consultancy, management research and all the rest of it) probably attended an old-fashioned and rather strict school in which the prevailing model was one of team spirit, pulling together, self-sacrifice, not letting the side down and fair internal competition under rigid, but explicit, rules; a world of order – mindless perhaps, and dependent, but above all, ordered.

Those who go simply to 'work' in order to live are much more likely to have attended a school which 'teaches', amongst other things, that the best you can do in this chaotic life is to survive, and you had better learn pretty soon to fight, either openly or, more likely, covertly, by opting out altogether. Later on, such people tend to be deaf to exhortations from management to 'all pull together' to combat a common external enemy (Japanese importers now, instead of 'St Custards'). The only 'club' available to the workers is called a union and the enemy is plainly close at hand.

The really important point is that 'management', in its club-like manifestations, reinforces the social splits already buried in the hearts and minds of those who work in despised 'industry'. Now all this is easier to see in Britain, because the British have made social class an art-form, but it is present just the same, reinforced by the English language, in American and Australian industry, and elsewhere in the old colonies.

I hope the reader will forgive my dwelling so long on the linguistics of management. The wonder for me is that anyone can set out to write about it at all without making it perfectly clear beforehand what he means, or at least, what his difficulties are in making sense of it. In this book, whenever there is any doubt, I propose to use the following nomenclature:

The meanings of management (3)

Management I = *activity* of running things; work.

Management II = *ideology* of management; values, assumptions.

Management III = *people*; a body of 'managers', paid to run things.

This classification of the meanings of the modern concept of management absorbs the earlier definitions. It is only in the twentieth century that Management I and Management III have a realistic existence, firstly because of an increase in the number of managers in bigger and more complicated organizations and secondly because academical folk began to think about what it was that a 'manager' actually did and how it differed from what other people did (such as workers and owners). Management II absorbed both the hermaphroditism and the status implications of earlier definitions. Management II, it should be noted is largely a phenomenon of British, British colonial and American work cultures.

---

2 The rise of the British manager

(From Sir Francis Drake to the Second World War)

1 The respectable buccaneer – the British proto-manager

Any observation of the word 'manager' must show it is not a simple concept; that it means different things to different people and that it has meant different things at different times. Who was the first manager? There is an old joke in consultancy circles that Jethro was the first management consultant:

(To Moses): 'The thing that thou doest is not good . . . thou wilt surely wear away . . . for this thing is too heavy for thee . . . hearken now unto my voice, I will give thee counsel . . . thou shalt provide out of all the people able men . . . and place such over them to be rulers of thousands, and rulers of hundreds, rulers of fifties, and rulers of ten . . . and it shall be that every great matter they shall bring unto thee, but every small matter they shall judge: so shall it be easier for thyself.' (Exodus, XVIII.)

But, management in its coping sense knows no historical barriers; all men are *all* managers and have always been so. However, in the narrower, technical sense, it might be right to look for an archetypal manager of the modern type at around the time that the word took on its modern meaning. We have noted that at the beginning of the sixteenth century the idea of managing had been extended to operations of war, and more generally, to taking charge of any sort of enterprise at all.

Let us begin with Francis Drake (later Sir Francis Drake), a sixteenth-century man with uncommon affinities with modern business. I list twenty-four facets of the man, in roughly the order they must have become apparent to his contemporaries. Virtually all of them he shares with the classic American *entrepreneurs* – unsurprising, as he lived when British entrepreneurship was in flower. (Why, as a matter of interest, did we have to borrow the word *entrepreneur* from the French?):

1 Humble origin. (As a matter of fact, Drake's father was a preacher and not badly connected, but Drake always acted out the poor-boy-made-good image. Frank Sinatra, a comparable success story, did the same thing, though his father was a lieutenant in the fire brigade – roughly the same sort of status, in fact, as Lieutenant Kojak.)

2 Impecunious father, unable to provide security, to control the family boundary, with consequent ingestion of feelings of frustration and rage. (Most of the great *entrepreneurs* come from this sort of background. The underlying need is not for money – as a love surrogate – or for power, *per se*, but for a sense of *control* over a naughty world. Most, like Sinatra, collect an entourage around them as a buffer against the exigencies of life in the real.)

3 Early experience of persecution as member of a *minority group*; that is, a Lutheran Protestant in the Catholic West Country. From the age of eight, Drake knew no stable home, being forced, because of his father's religion, to pass some of his formative years living on a beached ship.

4 Hard, character-building, apprenticeship in mastery of a particular skill (in his case seamanship in small, manoeuvreable boats, a skill which was to be of vast historical importance in the succeeding years).

5 A succession of patrons at crucial points of his career.

6 The first, crucial, lucky break – when Drake was about thirteen, his father was compelled 'by reason of his poverty to put his son to the master of a bark, with which he used to coast along the shore, and sometimes to carry merchandise into Zeeland and France. The youth, being painful and diligent, so pleased the old man by his industry, that, being a bachelor, at his death he bequeathed his bark unto him by will and testament.'

7 Short of stature.

8 Totally magnetic personality.

9 Boundless capacity for hard work.

10 Violent temper.

11 Coolly calculated courage.

12 Sense of mission allied to ambition. 'A sword in one hand, a Bible in the other and a good eye to the main chance.'

13 The classic break from the employee role at age thirty – i.e. going freelance.

14 The period in the wilderness after the first significant failure. (No one really knows where Drake spent the years between thirty-two and thirty-four years of age, but, hindsight suggests that, wherever it was, he

was girding his loins, psychologically, for what was to come.)

15 The breakthrough into creative mid-life (between thirty-six and forty). He met the Queen for the first time, pulled off his first big financial coup (the treasure ship *Cacafuego*) and circumnavigated the globe.

16 At forty, he became landed (Buckland Abbey, near Plymouth) and ennobled, the first of a long succession of newly-respectable business buccaneers to be so.

17 Preservation of the common touch throughout; the first broadly visible model of 'man-management'.

18 Persistent incapacity to cope with organizational superiors and peers (though not subordinates).

19 Love of display, ostentation and, most of all, flattery.

20 Possibly paranoid hounding of perceived traitors to him (Doughty, Borough, Fletcher).

21 Autocratic management style disguised as participative management: 'He has nine or ten gentlemen with him, members of good families in England, who are members of his council. On every occasion, however unimportant, he calls them together and listens to what they have to say before giving his orders – although, in fact, he pays no real attention to any one.' (Comment of the Spanish captain Don Francisco Zarate, captured by Drake in 1579.)

22 Wives kept firmly in their place and the obligatory young, beautiful and rich second wife taken when he was forty-four.

23 Growing inability to adapt to large-scale organization in the new era of the big squadrons and combined naval/military operations.

24 Political influence. Example: as MP Chairman of a parliamentary committee to discuss a bill to ban his entering the flour milling business by erecting six mills on the Plymouth water supply system. Needless to say, the bill failed in committee. Drake had, in fact, constructed the water system in the first place and had a sixty-seven-year lease for his milling operation built into the contract!

Why choose Drake as the British proto-manager? Part of his importance lies in the extent to which he was a beloved, national figure. Because his enterprises coincided with the national boundary, he became the embodiment of England in precisely the same way as Churchill in World War II. The Crown provided dependency for the populace and Drake carried the fight to a foreign bogeyman (Philip II) every bit as menacing as Hitler. The parallels are uncanny, even to the inhabitants of Sussex and Kent having (pre-television) ringside seats for the crucial engagement of the war – the definitive repulse of the foreign horde by lighter, pluckier, and more manoeuvreable craft. Of course, Drake was no bureaucrat manager in a big organization, but so popular was he that the model of management he represented must have been ingested by large parts of the population almost at the level of a moral lesson.

What was that lesson? In the first place, it taught that you can't really do anything through the system. The idea of the rugged individualist, so dear to modern Englishmen in their dealings with local authorities etc., was imprinted by Drake and especially by his officially independent position. But, of course, it was never quite so. Drake, officially in disgrace after his marauding on the Spanish Main in 1579 was nonetheless summoned by the Queen out of her interest in the 'curiosities' he had managed to collect on his voyage around the world. All we know for sure is *all* the treasure went forthwith to the Tower of London for safekeeping and that ever since, though not necessarily causally, Englishmen have shown a marked distaste for submitting themselves to formal embodiments of the common good – the 'State'.

The second fundamental lesson must have been that if you happen to make a lot of money dishonestly, you can get to keep quite a lot of it if your connections are good enough. In fact, if enough of it gets funnelled into the appropriate sources of patronage, you can be reasonably certain of some form of ennoblement in due course and, hence, respectability. The lesson seems to have gone deep and may easily be observed today in the British 'honours' system. One of the continuing puzzles about that extraordinary institution, the City of London, is the regularity with which apparently intelligent merchant bankers and those of their ilk are taken in by the most transparently crooked con-men, often of alien origin. Why, we must ask, is this so, and how is it that the lesson never seems to be learned? What underlying assumption about their role and function drops them in the muck almost every time? The answer is fundamentally simple; the average Englishmen believes that if you are going to make a lot of money, if you *sincerely* want to be rich, it cannot be done in total honesty. Accordingly, if you wish (quite rightly) to obtain the maximum gain for your clients' money, it makes perfect sense to direct it towards a plausible finger-man who looks, on the whole, likely to get away with whatever it is he is cooking up.

My attention was drawn to this phenomenon by a journalist colleague who interviewed, before the truth hit the fan, one of the more celebrated rogues of recent years. My friend knew nothing of the particular business of this man and little of his background and yet it was perfectly clear to him within a few moments of his arrival that he was in the presence of a spectacular crook. He claims in fact to have had to restrain an impulse to check his wallet on his departure, so powerful was this impression. How, he asked himself, could anyone be taken in by such a man? Of course, it was the wrong question. For the City, the man in question was seen as some kind of wizard; his enterprise, on paper, was so much more profitable than any of its competitors that he *had* to have magical powers; if not, he would have to be a crook. He *was* a crook of course, and the thing blew up a couple of years later, hurting no one but legions of shareholders who probably shared the merchant bankers' value system in all respects.

To Drake, more than anyone, we owe this legacy, and to the society that nurtured him. There was really no one quite like Drake in Continental Europe and there would not be for another two hundred years. The respectable buccaneer is a product of an expanding, imperialistic culture, just as the legend of Robin Hood (do other cultures have Robin Hoods?) was a product of an oppressively hierarchical one. The urge towards wealth and dominance simply has to be rationalized somehow, because somebody is going to have a conscience about it all. Nowadays, in a world of bigness, the exact parallel would be the American planemakers bribing their way around the globe under the benevolent eye of the Nixon administration. No one actually *knew* (anymore than Queen Elizabeth I) what was going on and yet, no one could doubt it. Drake, in sociologists' jargon, was the quintessence of the up-

ward socially-mobile; and business, in Britain as elsewhere, is where you achieve social mobility through wealth. The principle of the respectable buccaneer provides us with an example of temporal binary thought. That is, the split between the clean and dirty times in the entrepreneurial career. Just as there are clean and dirty places to be, and roles to fill, so there may be in a country like Britain an utterly dirty phase transformed, in the second half of life, into utter respectability. In other cultures, you might be expected to be *reasonably* honest throughout if you wish to be in a state of grace by the end. To put it in modern terms, Drake was 'on a fiddle' – a sort of accidentally done-a-purpose form of crookedry, deplored, but half-indulged at the same time. I am not a good enough linguist to be sure that 'fiddle' translates satisfactorily into other languages; I doubt it.

2 The agent

While Drake was clearly a fine exponent of Management I (i.e. running things), most people would regard him as an *entrepreneur*, as though that was entirely something else. It was probably towards the end of the eighteenth century that the idea of managing, as a process, began to be specialized to the idea of a collective body of men and hence to the *job* of manager. It appears to have happened first in the theatre, newspapers and workhouses, although what logic there may be for this is difficult to determine. Possibly, these were simply new, or newly enlarged types of institution wherein it became obvious that what had to be done was different from 'administration' as the word was commonly understood. No doubt, in these fields, that which had to be managed was felt to be relatively volatile and unpredictable, just like a horse is inclined to be. In addition, all of them are institutions in which people, to some extent, represent the dominant throughput, as compared with manufacturing industry. It was not long however before the word was borrowed by manufacturing industry to soften the nineteenth-century distinction between *masters* and men. In essence, it described the functions of an *agent* (for the owners) in an organization which had become too big to be controlled directly and whose owners, anyway, probably did not wish to be reminded too frequently what they were doing to the communities which housed their factories. Nothing much has changed; now we talk of 'middle management' as distinct from senior or executive management. Top management, as Galbraith has pointed out, has largely, together with the mysterious institutional investors and pension fund managers, supplanted the old owner.

Middleness is, in fact, a *function* of size. Perhaps the single most important change in the recent history of work is the rise of the large organization or bureaucracy. The Church, Civil Service and Army apart, there had simply not been really big work organizations before the end of the nineteenth century, and we cannot be said to have got the hang of them yet. In fact, in the 'small is beautiful' era, we seem to be losing

'Them' and 'us' in the big organization

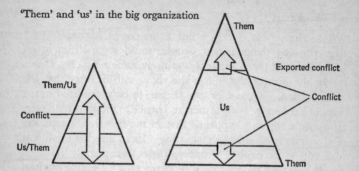

our enthusiasm for them fast. These are the 'intermediate' institutions between the State (plus its various bureaucracies) and the local organizations (e.g., boroughs, villages) with which we may feel some sense of contact or affinity.

The likely casualty of the big bureaucracies or corporations is the men and women in the middle. There is no particular identity to middle management work *except* that it stands in between those who matter at the top and those who matter at the bottom of the organizational hierarchy. Furthermore, those at the top and bottom are actually in touch with the organizational environment, that is, with employees (otherwise known as members of the community), raw materials and finished products or, in the stratosphere, with merchant bankers, politicians and the heads of other enterprises. Who do middle managers deal with? Other middle managers mostly, but functionally they are there to provide a buffer between the binary extremes. In doing so they act *for* top management and aspire *to* top management. It is a role structurally indistinguishable from the eighteenth- and nineteenth-century agent except that, instead of having for a boss an *owner* with a vague responsibility to the local community, you have a higher-level boss with a vague responsibility to the Board of Directors with a vague responsibility to the community. Acting as agent for those above and lost in the internal logic of the bureaucracy, the middle manager often finds it hard to grasp that those who work under him are actually *members* of the community –

wearing, for the moment, the hat of *employee*. He may even find it hard to grasp that those employees are entitled at work to exactly the same sort of constitutional rights to a say in things and a source of redress as they have come to expect in the role of citizen.

Because middle managers find it hard to identify with what the organization is fighting for and because most of them become over-dependent on their employers, their primary concern is career survival. Thus they take up safe and ultra-cautious postures in the organization, projecting conflict outwards and polarizing it into senior management and workers and their representatives. For all the talk of 'professional management' over the years, the central issue for *middle* managers remains one of client identification. You can't realistically apply 'professional' criteria without the test of service versus clients and it is made doubly difficult if such criteria play no part in career selection and preferment. Encased in the large organization, the middle manager is largely without that test, and that has been the case ever since organizations got really big and agents started to be styled 'managers'.

The long downhill slope Before we consider the manager in his modern manifestations, one central fact has to be taken account of and that is the steady decline of British industrial fortunes since the 1830s. This is a somewhat contentious point, because most observers have assumed that, as the peak of the boom occurred in mid-Victorian times, the beginnings of a decline must be dated to nearer the end of the nineteenth century. If it can be shown that the latter half of the nineteenth century in fact represents not only a financial boom, but also the beginnings of a process of rationalizing failure, then our whole historical perspective must be altered and our view of 'management' and the emergent management philosophies within it. Is there, in other words, a link between the rationalization of decline and the emergence of a 'management' movement?

Hobsbawm and Barnett, amongst others, have assembled impressive evidence about the true timing of industrial decline and about its obviousness to informed commentators throughout. For example, although at the end of the nineteenth century Britain exceeded all other countries in the volume and value of her exports, it had already become clear that her industrial education and the rate of effective application of science to industry had fallen behind Continental Europe. Moreover, Britain was bound to be overtaken quickly by other nations unless there were (to quote Richard Cobden in 1835!) a 'timely remodelling of our system; so as to put it as nearly as possible upon an equality with the improved management of the Americans.' The quote above is important both as the harbinger of countless almost identical statements from that day to this, but also because it may represent the beginnings of a special relationship, of the love/hate variety, with American industry. To the informed, at any rate, it was clear that the Americans knew how to do it and the British, increasingly, did not. Then, in 1867, the Paris Exhibition created consternation in Britain as so many of the prizes for quality products were carried off by Continental manufacturers, particularly the French. That shock led to the creation of seven new technical colleges in the succeeding years, deriving from the Mechanics Institutes and promoted and funded by provincial business-men. But there things languished until World War I. The really significant changes in British education had to wait another seventy years. It has been said that the crucial dif-ference between Britain and Germany in this regard is that in Germany the educational revolution *preceded* the industrial revolution rather than vice versa.

This is not the place to detail the arguments about 'the sudden transformation of the leading and most dynamic industrial economy into the most sluggish and conservative, in the short space of thirty to forty years'. Hobsbawm argues that Britain's early entry into industrialization, together with her distinctive and traditional pattern of world-wide trading links, cushioned her from the necessity of moving into the second, science-based, phase of industrialization. In short, it was uniquely possible for British industrialists and traders to go on making money (and becoming respectable) through old processes and old colonial markets, without recourse to costly and awkward developments of technological method. 'In Britain, there was never the slightest general shortage of capital, given the country's wealth and the relative cheapness of the early industrial processes, but a large section of those who benefitted from this diversion of income – and the richest among them in particular – invested their money *outside* direct industrial development, or wasted it, thus forcing the rest of the (smaller) *entrepreneurs* to press even more harshly upon labour.'

Through all the upheavals of industrialization, the split-off respectable side of British society remained largely untouched, a gentle and pleasant haven for all who could afford the entry fee. 'Placid and prosperous were the lives of the numerous parasites of rural aristocratic society, high and low – that rural and small-town world of functionaries of and suppliers to the nobility and gentry, and the traditional, somnolent, corrupt and, as the industrial revolution proceeded, increasingly reactionary professions . . . The lawyers, and what passed for a civil service, were unreformed and unregenerate . . . Above all, the merchant and financier – especially the merchant involved in overseas trade . . . remained the most respected and most crucial form of *entrepreneur* long after the mills, factories and foundries covered the northern skies with smoke and fog.' Thus, there was a binary split of clean and dirty occupations, clean and dirty geographic places and, in aspiration, a well-regulated process by which one could graduate from the dirty to the clean chapters of life itself.

By the end of the nineteenth century, the newspapers had taken up a 'wake up England' theme, in a series of depressingly familiar-looking analyses of British industry vis-à-vis its Continental and American competitors. By 1915, in the mobilization for World War I, it turned out that Britain produced *half* the quantity of steel of German industry and then in neither the quality nor specialized kinds needed. (Both the USA and Germany had overtaken British steel production between 1890 and 1895!) The official history of the Ministry of Munitions says:

British manufacturers were behind other countries in research, plant and method. Many of the iron and steel firms were working on a small scale, old systems and uneconomical plant . . . The British machine toolmaker was conservative both as regards novelty in design and quality of output.

Britain had in fact become reliant on the USA and Germany for the most modern machine tools and on Germany also for ball bearings and magnetos, laboratory instruments, gauges, optical glass and many other essential goods, including most chemicals. ICI is, in fact, the product of the wartime creation of a chemical industry, together with the subsequent seizure of German patents. By the 1930s, Germany had grabbed half the world trade in machine tools whereas the British share had shrunk to seven per cent. In the years before World War II Britain had to buy Swiss, German, Hungarian and American machine tools in order to rearm at all.

'Because we had almost no clock or instrument industry, the early marks of Hurricane and Spitfire had to be fitted with Swiss and American instrumentation. The Swiss provided the fuses for our shells and so the catalogue went on . . . ' (Barnett.)

Now, the extraordinary thing about these truths lies not so much in their obviousness to informed observers over a period of nearly 150 years, but the extent to which the populace at large has declined to recognize them. The penny, somewhat devalued, seems to have dropped only in the last few years and, arguably, since the Hudson Institute's much vaunted exercise in extrapolation led to the perfectly natural long-term comparison of Britain with the world-position of Portugal! It may be that so long as Britain could feel herself to be in the major leagues, though acknowledged as slipping within them, some kind of process of rationalization could continue; but – Portugal! that was another kind of referent, another league altogether. The keen-eyed observer will have noticed that there is an almost exact historical correlation between the accelerated decline of British industrial fortunes and the emergence of the British management movement. I am not positing a causal link; simply noting the coincidence in the context of the German, French and Swedish capacity to manage successfully without an accompanying philosophical 'movement' or a separate management specialism.

If the central features of recent British industrial history are decline and the rationalization of decline, how can this be explained – what happened to all that *energy* that characterized the original industrial revolution? Most romantics think of the industrial revolution as, in some respects at least, a creative moment of history – a major discontinuity brought about by the genius of man. Even the Victorian working classes, as Raymond Williams reminds us, were captured, in the midst of poverty and exploitation, by the wonder of it all, just as admiring lunatics may now be found, directly under the Concorde flight path, marvelling at the thing while the fabric of their houses crumbles around them. But at the centre of British society, the dominant motive for several hundred years has been *money* and hence greed. The supreme irony of recent times has been the decline of many of the old and greedy Colonial powers, Britain included, in favour of the sober and puritan Germans, Americans and Swedes. Thus, Francis Drake as proto-manager: make your money, sailing as close to the wind as you dare and get out (to the country) so the offspring may live like gentlemen; but elsewhere, the second generation would probably go into the business expecting to leave it twice as big. (In France, seven out of the ten biggest firms remain substantially in family control – another little-known, but highly significant, statistic.) The greater wonder is not the economic decline of Britain, but the astonishing artifice with which old reserves of materials, cash, know-how, human resources and good will have been eked out over the years by a tiny island full of agreeably indolent romantics. As Raymond Williams comments in *The Country and the City*, the Colonies *were* effectively 'country' to a new urban state which had not been self-sufficient in food since about 1850. When the cheap raw materials began to dry up, there was still the massive outflow of capital to provide an income-base, though a short-lived one.

If greed has been at the heart of British piracy, trade and industry, in that order, for 300 years, its inevitable legacy, after its effects in the industrial revolution, was *revulsion*. The effects of industrialization (or, more correctly, the effects of owners not really regarding 'labour' as people at all, interposing 'managers' to carry the can) ran nowhere so deep as in Britain; the proletariatization of the workforce was nowhere else so completely achieved. In the industrial revolution, greed drove out common sense and with it the last hope of a reintegration of the populace in the purposes and ideology of industry. The revulsion was non-specific, almost random; the scapegoat was not to be greed itself but the industrialists, their agents, the products they made, the process of manufacture – indeed industry itself.

To be sure, it was no long-term benefit to have been first to industrialize. For one thing, this fact may account for the fundamental and enduring anti-intellectualism of British industry. Even today, industrialists refer to 'theory', as though it had nothing to do with practice and vice versa – 'academic' is almost the ultimate sneer. At just the point that Continental educational institutions were beginning to theorize about the new industrial processes and techniques, the British *entrepreneurs* and engineers were moving into second-phase improvization of a severely and typically British kind. 'If the boiler blew up, you strapped another band round it; if the bridge collapsed, you bolted on more, and thicker, cast-iron next time. Our *entrepreneurs* built their businesses by similar commercial methods, starting small as a local tradesman or craftsman, and expanding by grace of native nous. Equally the men who actually constructed the early machines and operated the early mechanized processes were traditional craftsmen who learned how to do the new things as they went along, and passed on their knowledge verbally to their apprentices . . . There was (therefore) in British industry, right from the start, a tradition of the resourceful amateur, self-taught on job, rather than the man specially and elaborately trained. This was true all the way from the Board Room to the bench.' (Barnett.)

Clearly, the peculiar character of British educational institutions played a part in this. Part of this is probably attributable to the late-eighteenth-century and early-nineteenth-century religious revival, beginning with Wesley and Whitfield. The new non-conformist religions, in their concern for the individual soul, reinforced the prevailing individualistic picture of man; a romantic, other-worldly picture, remote from the emergent realities of economic and industrial life. The lingering British trust in the absolute freedom of the individual to be king in his own castle undermined the attempts of some to bring about a timely concentration in British industry; whereas, by the turn of the century, all manner of powerful cartels and trusts had sprung up in the USA and Germany.

High religious idealism is not inherently incompatible with the achievement of commercial and industrial sucess – the English simply *believed*, after over 200 years of various forms of piracy, that they were incompatible. Two quotes give the clue to the nineteenth-century picture of education. Firstly, a JP writing in 1807 of the education of the poor: 'It is doubtless desirable that the poor should be generally instructed in *reading*, if it were only for the best of purposes – that they may read the Scriptures. As to *writing* and *arithmetic*, it may be apprehended that such a degree of knowledge would produce in them a disrelish for the laborious occupations of life.' Note also, inevitably, Dr Arnold of Rugby, on the sort of boys *he* got to teach: 'Rather than have science the principal thing in my son's mind, I would gladly have him think the sun went round the earth and that the stars were so many spangles set in the bright blue firmament. Surely, the one thing needed for a Christian and Englishman to study is a Christian and moral philosophy.' In their way, these are eminently sensible statements. The problem is the binary, either-or construction. There was no conception that a true 'all-round man' might combine head, hands, heart and guts in the one skin; that he might be inspired by the highest ideals *and* know how to work a lathe.

Also, education could not cope with the phenomenal population increase of the nineteenth century and especially the concentration of population in the towns. The debate on education was rather arid and necessarily binary in character, largely as a result of the fact that the grammar schools were already funnelling away middle-class university entrants destined for the old professions as well as for the army and civil service. There were three basic groups conducting the debate on nineteenth-century education – the public educators, the industrial trainers and the old humanists:

In general, the curriculum which the nineteenth century evolved can be seen as a compromise between all three groups, but with the industrial trainers predominant. The significant case is the long controversy over science and technical education. If we look at the range of scientific discovery between the seventeenth and the end of the nineteenth centuries, it is clear that its importance lies only in part in its transformation of the techniques of production and communication; indeed lies equally in its transformation of man's view of himself and of his world. Yet the decisive educational interpretation of this new knowledge was not in terms of its essential contribution to liberal studies, but in terms of *technical training for a particular class of men*. The old humanists muddled the issue by claiming a fundamental distinction between their traditional learning and that of the new disciplines, and it was from this kind of thinking that there developed the absurd defensive reaction that all real learning was undertaken without thought of practical advantage. (Williams.)

Here again we see the binary mode of thinking, the splitting of science into pure and applied and the simultaneous splitting of education into its clean (professional) and sullied (industrial) components.

By 1913 – 'There was no compelling reason why Britain had only 9000 university students compared with almost 60,000 in Germany; or only five day students per 10,000 (in 1900) compared with almost thirteen in the USA; why Germany produced 300 graduate engineers per annum compared, in England and Wales, with only 350 graduates in *all* branches of science, technology and mathematics with first or second class honours; and few of these were qualified for research.' (Hobsbawm.) Today, the Oxbridge graduate is still predominant in the boardrooms of the bigger British organizations, proportionate to those with a grounding in the essential technological and manufacturing processes of industry. One observer of managerial thinking processes suggests that even today, archaic modes of thought prevail – 'make a debating point, support it and don't make a logical error. It goes back to the days when the church controlled education and its main purpose was to preserve its ideology. Theology, being a structured system, has to be watertight for, if someone can knock a single hole in it, the whole thing collapses. This whole business of devoting our intellectual resources to "knocking a hole in it" means that we think that, if we can show a chap is wrong on one of his speculations, we can sit back and say, "I have demolished it". Whereas, an idea which is 40% balls and 60% sound is useful'. Hardly anyone really wants to go into industry (on the wrong side of the binary respectability line) and, those that do, often approach it according to thought patterns more appropriate to clergymen and dons (on the right side). That is a product both of industrial decline and the persistence of irrelevant assumptions about the nature of education.

3 The Quaker as manager

(*The belated discovery of industrial morals*) From the start, the great Quaker and Quaker-influenced firms – the Rowntrees, the Cadburys, the Levers, Mather & Platt, Renolds, Cammell Laird and so on, gave the lie to the peculiar British notion that morality and profit are mutually exclusive. From the early nineteenth century a minority of firms had gone in for various good works aimed at improving the welfare of workers – model villages, public baths, recreational clubs, libraries – at the same time sustaining a paternalistic vision of a kind of extended family. These schemes usually stemmed from religious conviction, rather than any idea of corporate effectiveness, and they appear sometimes to have incurred appreciable losses for the employers. However, by the end of the nineteenth century, the Quaker firms and the managers who worked for them had moved to some perception that treating people as if they were really people, rather than inert elements drawn from a 'labour market' might even be good business. Thus, by the turn of the century, regular training schemes, high wage policies, below-average hours of work, improved communications procedures and even joint consultation had all found some place in these few enlightened firms.

Here, as elsewhere, Britain led the world. But, here, as elsewhere, the creative minority remained a split-off particle of the British industrial whole. The remarkable thing was not the existence of these practices at all, but the extraordinary way in which other firms were untouched by them, as though the whole thing were simply some kind of religious aberration. Realistically, the Quakers were, and are, pretty hard-headed businessmen, standing on the middle ground between high-blown morality and heartless manipulation. For example, they always saw women as *people*, just as likely to be skilful and resourceful as men, and certainly entitled to the same rights – a *very* eccentric view in Victorian England. But, historically, the Quakers are a freak. They were *for* efficiency, for its own sake and for moral reasons but, nonetheless, they saw through the crude 'engineering' approach to industrial effectiveness which became associated with some sectors of American industry.

The point really is that industry had already become fixed in the public mind as a 'hard' domain. Thus, in the best traditions of binary thought, the soft employers had subconsciously to be split off from the mainstream lest they contaminate others with their effete and debilitating practices. The splitting off of the Quaker firms would be a suitable topic for research. In fact, the research industry has devoted very little attention to success stories – that is, those organizations which have embodied a set of values *and* also made high-quality products, to specification, on time, profitably. There are many such organizations and they all seem to have the same kind of chief executive.

4 The manager as middle-man

(*The 'professional' Mk. 1*) I have made reference, elsewhere, to a number of binary splits in British management thought. The argument certainly can be made that a split, class society existed in a unique way in Britain compared with the rest of the industrialized world, a function of, amongst other things, the virtual disappearance of a peasantry and its replacement by an urban proletariat. More contentious is the suggestion that the binary splits of thought and structure in British society p. 18) – class, geographic, urban/rural, political, are *symptoms* of a peculiar binary cast of thought – a virtual intolerance of the complexity and ambiguity of the middle ground. The most striking example is the survival of the two-party political system, a survival which, in complex times, has turned political statement into mindless ritual. After the war, all over Europe (though not in the USA), all manner of coalitions and amalgamations were the rule and not illogically so.

My own experience as a consultant supports this contention; in particular, what seems to me as the characteristic British approach to *not* taking difficult decisions. A group of American businessmen will fight out the issues at length, until the chairman says, 'OK, we've talked enough – we'll do this!' And so they do. If it is a truly difficult decision, the superficial British pattern will be similar, except that the committee will somehow contrive to split 50/50, thus ensuring a postponement of the decision or, more likely, the taking of a decision which turns out not to be a decision after all; two weeks later: 'I thought we decided that?' – 'Well, there's going to be another meeting.' It is, of course, a way of having decisions taken for you, a position which I have characterized elsewhere as the *dependent* one. The ducking or postponement of difficult decisions is not, of course, the exclusive preserve of the British, but it is exactly what you would expect in a culture of 'absent leadership' oriented towards relationships rather than outputs. (See Chapter 3.)

The emergence of the 'professional' management movement in the UK and the USA, at the beginning of the twentieth century, has to be seen in this context because nothing like it occurred in Continental Europe. The essential appeal of the 'professional' manager was that he would hold the middle ground between the poles of ownership and labour. The manager, whatever he had been before, was being pushed into centre-stage as the 'third-force' – the shock absorber between the irresistible force and the immovable object. Of course, in a binary setting, to attempt to hold the middle ground is to be shoved, or tugged, in one direction or another, or, if you are particularly resolute, to run the risk of being torn apart.

Now, borrowing from the Quakers, the idea of industry as a 'national service' began to emerge, together with the linked idea of managerial stewardship – the manager as a 'professional'. Once again, the contrast with Germany is apt; the Germans do not have a word for 'professional' in the class sense, any more than they have a word for 'management'. Other evidence suggests that ideas about a third force, about 'professionalism' in pursuit of 'national service' represented for some a grand-sounding way of describing union-bashing. John Child argues that, in the 1920s, the phenomenal operating *definition* of management (that is, the definition you arrive at by observing what people *did* rather than what they *said*) was the amelioration of labour conflict. In the slump of course, the scales of power had swung strongly away from the unions and it is difficult to resist the conclusion that, in the end, the new 'professional' manager was little more than the old agent/manager dressed up in Quaker livery.

This may seem to be an unkind reflection of the management thinkers of the time, some of whom (Lee, Sheldon, Bowie) had proved extraordinarily far-sighted. Somewhat depressingly, modern versions of 'industrial democracy' are barely distinguishable from the views of these 1920s writers; depressingly, not because the ideas have no merit but because they seem to so many people to be so new. The point is that what these thinkers had to say (the British writers, pre-Elton Mayo, were ahead of American thought) was no more integrated into practice than the accurate prohecies of the doom-sayers or the true wisdom of the Quakers. Industry remained the domain of the hard, 'practical' man, living for the present.

Writers complained bitterly of industry's indifference to the development of new ideas and concepts. Bowie, for example, could in 1930 chastise the great bulk of British employers, particularly those in the coal, iron and steel, cotton, woollen, pottery, and gas industries, for their conservative individualism, opposition to business education, ignorance of research findings, nepotism, and secretiveness. And certainly the attempts of many employers in this period to cut wage-rates and

lengthen hours of work in a desperate search for lower costs were completely at variance with those elementary lessons of industrial psychology
which had long been absorbed by the management intellectuals. (Child.)

It was in the 1920s also that we see an early demonstration of
'catch-22' in practice. It followed naturally from the idea of
'professionalism' that there should be a professional society,
duly founded as the Institute of Industrial Administration in
1920. It followed naturally from *this*, that there should be a
determined effort to improve standards of management and
that meant the provision of education to help with the new
challenges of post-war industry. The logic then ran that you
had to have recruits to management capable of benefitting
from the new management education and hence of a certain
minimum educational qualification. But, the presenting problem
was labour and the perceived inequity of reward and opportunity. Thus, by building management and management
education on a foundation of selective entry – the 'closed shop'
idea later to be expounded by Bowie – the main problem for
management – the very *reason for its existence* was, inevitably,
exacerbated. Management as a third force was supposed to
hold the balance, but, by now 'management' as an occupation
had become a primary route of upward mobility and thus a
reinforcement of the original split. Again, the astonishing
thing is not this very absurdity, but the fact that no one at the
time appears to have noticed it.

While the professional management movement was getting
under way (a process which began progressively to seal off
British management thought from practice on the Continent)
two other linked manifestations of the manager emerged, each
in their way propping up the 'professional' idea.

5 The manager as 'scientist'

(*The scientific management movement*) All professions are supposed
to have a 'science', a body of arcane knowledge on which they
are based and which distinguishes them from other callings.
If the agents of the owners required legitimation for what they
were up to, then they needed a 'profession', but they could not

have a profession, of the traditional type, without a science. So, the hunt was on for some set of 'principles' of management to justify the existence of a profession in the first place. Like the snark, the principles have proved an elusive quarry, although the hunt is still on sixty years later. The notion of a management science brought with it two problems:

1 It reversed the process by which professions had traditionally emerged – i.e.:
traditional: Identification of specialized activity'– formation of profession – establishment of standards for legitimation.
'management': Demand for legitimation – formation of profession – hunt for specialized activity.
2 It intensified the splitting-off of management from life. In other words, in what sense does any man or woman *cease* to manage in normal life? How can the activity of running things, to put it at its crudest, be separated out from the process of life itself?

The correct questions to ask in relation to management science in the context of executive work are:

1 Do business executives act in a predictable enough way for their work to be treated in an accepted scientific manner by outside observers?
2 Are they really scientists of a kind through the nature of the work they do?
3 Do they use the techniques of management science consistently and successfully in the normal course of their work?

The answers to all these questions are not much clearer now than they were between the wars, although since the pioneering studies of Sune Carlson (then at the Stockholm School of Economics) in the 1940s, the manager as he *is* has become a serious focus of study, rather than the fantasy manager/scientist of the 1920s and 30s. Most of the evidence suggests that real management work is characterized by variety, discontinuity and brevity. Managers work in power networks, armed with informal information and at high speed. Decision-making, one of the main planks of the rational/scientific management idea, tends to be done through the seat of the pants, or off the top of the head, or in some other place, but rarely in an orderly, 'scientific' fashion. Most senior executives, Carlson found, cling fondly to an idea of a 'typical' day which never, or hardly ever, actually happens. That is to say that a lot of time is spent in frenetic pursuits which executives do not really regard as part of their highly-organized and calm decision-making job, even though they do it all the time, year after year. To put it more bluntly, there is a mythology about executive work, sedulously nourished by the management consultants, business school professors, and so on. Executives like the myth and are prepared to pay good money to have it reinforced. But if top executives are not prepared to deal with reality, as opposed to fantasy, God help us all.

Contrast the reality with Sheldon, writing in 1923: 'Management is no longer the wielding of the whip; it is rather the delving into experience and the building upon facts. Its leadership is based upon knowledge rather than upon force. Its task is no longer solely that of "getting the job through" rather, in many of its activities, it operates through the application of a capacity trained in the investigation and solution of problems. Management, in fact, instead of being a law unto itself, has found that there are laws which it must obey.'

Later on, Colonel Urwick, effortlessly transcribing the order of the army to the conduct of business, wrote *The Principles of Direction and Control* in 1928. Here, the idea of an organization as a pyramid of concrete blocks, scientifically constructed, reached its apogee. The span of human control could, for example, be specified, as if the whole edifice would wobble to the ground if one of the beams were overloaded. 'It is possible to lay down certain principles and guides to action which are valid in *all* cases.'

6 The manager as quisling

(or the manager in the role of pal.) The scientific management idea began to die of natural causes in the 1930s. During the slump, and particularly after the collapse of the British general strike

in 1926, scientific management seemed to make sense; after all, the main imponderable (labour conflict) was not, for the moment, entirely imponderable – if the most volatile element in the mix can be rendered inert, then a physical sciences model of control and predictability may seem to be appropriate. However, it wasn't long before Human Relations came on the scene, much trumpeted as a replacement for scientism. Insofar as it turned the spotlight on people, that is, workers, it did represent a change. But, it was a change in much the same sense as the smooth supplanting of Chinese Confucianism by Communism at approximately the same time. The replacement of a religion by an anti-religion, or vice versa, looks, on the surface, to be a *volte-face*; but, under the skin, the cultural assumptions about conduct and especially about dependence remained as they had always been.

So it was with human relations. Once the unionists began to gather strength again the new stratagem was 'leadership', loosely translated as persuasion. The best way to outfox the unions was to render junior management more *persuasive*, better at selling notions of 'common purpose', 'teamwork', through 'leadership' and 'communications' (downwards, of course) and 'human relations skills'. Now the foreman and first-line manager were expected to absorb the shocks in exchange for the right of entry to the illusory brotherhood of 'management'. From then till now, management has shrunk away from recognizing the significance of the differences between the top and the bottom of increasingly long hierarchical chains of management. The chairman may earn a bit more, have a bigger office and rather more flunkeys but (please God) we are all managers together. Believing this, believing in the solidarity picture of organizational life, allowed the first-line managers to accept that really everybody's interests were as one in the end.

Apart from the concept of 'catch-22' itself, Joseph Heller's other great contribution to contemporary thought is the character of the classic *entrepreneur*, Milo Minderbinder, the archetype of American human relations – 'It's all in the syndicate and everybody has a share.' Milo took the solidarity ethic to its logical conclusion; it is all right to bomb your own base, provided it can be done profitably and everybody has a share. In fact, the basic notion of human relations had been alive and well in Britain in the 1920s, but it was only in its American packaging, particularly through Elton Mayo's Hawthorne experiments, that it caught hold in the 40s and 50s. Its essential lure was the implicit fantasy that industrial administration might be conflict-free (everybody has a share) *if only* people would cooperate and pull together, *if only* the 'whole person' could be engaged wholeheartedly in work, *if only* the foreman had 'leadership'. It was an agreeable, fantastic, 'if only' sort of world-view, in which the unions were necessarily cast as obdurate, destructive and reactionary; and so, in time, they became.

In human relations, technical performance was assumed to derive from the pursuit of what at first appeared to be an acceptable social goal – the increase of employee contentment. Only a more critical appraisal indicated how readily this system might entail the manipulation of employees at the expense of those who were chosen representatives of their material interests. In this way, human relations could be, and was, used to support a philosophy hostile to the organized labour movement. This placed it in contrast to the accommodating attitudes expressed in the Reconstruction period after 1918, and during the early 1920s. (Child.)

Again, nothing much has changed. One of the most celebrated and expensive behavioural science gurus of modern times puts it that management by 'movement' is dead and management by 'motivation' must replace it. This sounds moral enough, but loosely translated, it means that workers have wised up to the one (management by movement) and need outfoxing with something a lot cleverer (management by motivation, naturally). It is an alluring message for the naturally exploitive senior executive who wants also to sleep easy of nights. It is, in fact, a brutal distortion of the Quaker approach nearly a century before; they really believed in it all.

The cast so far

The analysis so far suggests that the 'manager' has been cast in a range of symbolic roles since Elizabethan times. The British proto-manager is a buccaneer, a symbol for getting away with it and good luck to him. The first true manager (in the Management III sense) – is, properly speaking, a mere agent, hence the reference earlier to 'mere manager'. But, more recently, management's symbolic roles have tended to multiply due, as I have suggested, to a multiplication of factors bearing on it; firstly, the reality of decline, secondly, the increase in size of organizations and hence of the actual numbers of managers and thirdly, and most importantly, the turning of society's face away from industry and all it had come to represent – brutalism, exploitation and anti-intellectualism.

It is in these multiple symbolic roles that we begin to detect something of the complexity of modern 'management'. The roles I have referred to as 'middleman' (the third party), 'scientist' and quisling (the human relations managers) emerged almost simultaneously as different facets of a process of attempted legitimation of a role which was held by society in generally low esteem. Child has pointed out that the technical and legitimatory threads of British management thought are always difficult to disentangle. Clearly, the appeal to professionalism, science and human relations (all good motherhood concepts) is linked with legitimation and yet each symbolic role represents, at the same time, realistic aspects of Management I, the *activity* of work in which managers engage. Bruce Reed, one of the more original thinkers about the subject, suggests that management, in modern times, must be thought of in terms of three interlinked types of activity:

The meanings of management (4)

1 Technician – that which is required to make the *company* system work (tasks, organization, selection, delegation, systems, reality-testing, risk-taking, efficiency).

2 Leader – that which is required to make relationships work (understanding of multiple roles and psychological need, followership [especially the distinction between employee, trade unionist and community roles], ego strength, nous to tell the difference between task and emotional survival types of behaviour, maturity to use emotion to cope with projected dependency and to fight where necessary.)

3 Trustee – that which is required to understand the connection between

management policy and decisions and the environment (awareness of the link of legal and political structures, awareness also of continuous interaction over the company boundary and the overlapping of company, negotiating and community structures, confidence to change role according to designated position in the relevant structure).

It can be seen that each of these realistic elements of Management I is paralleled, even parodied, by the legitimatory/symbolic roles of the inter-war years:
Technician = Scientific Manager
Leader   = Human Relations Manager
Trustee   = 'Professional' Manager

Thus, the symbolic roles were always rooted in reality but somehow they lost their innocence in time, partly because the new executive class went on behaving pretty much as the old owners had done, though more subtly, and partly because management education and management development soon obfuscated the simplest realities with new and ponderous languages only *some* of which were important to *some* of the more specialized managers. By World War II, management itself had started to become an unnecessarily complicated business, bearing in mind the inevitable, necessary complications of specialist areas such as chemistry, manufacturing technology and so on. On the surface, it is a paradox that so anti-intellectual an industrial sector should, in the end, spawn a management education edifice so much larger than was to be found on the Continent. But, by the time the war started, there was already a great deal of high-class technical education on the Continent, firmly rooted in the area of *Technik* and not masquerading as anything else.

The present and existing British professions were by and large an invention of the middle and late Victorian period, created for essentially social reasons but also to fill an educational vacuum. The new urban middle classes, increasingly powerful in an expanding and more complex economy, built up a series of new employee groups, self-regulating through the establishment of qualifying associations, and calling themselves 'professional' in order to increase their market capacity and enchance their claim to status. This was part of a 'scramble for professional status' on the part of competing groups, for whom job requirements were only one of several considerations. Three types of quantity surveyor were finally established and three main types of accountant. Engineers were the extreme example; today there are currently about forty qualifying bodies for engineers in Britain, fifteen being for those with graduate-level qualifications.

Continental practice saw no need for such groupings. In Europe the qualifying function has been retained by full-time education. So the diploma from a full-time course within formal university level education is the crucial piece of paper. British higher education was never forced to consider so fully the requirements of jobs, as an exam-giving professional body has always been there to act as a buffer. Instead of being qualifying associations, French, Swedish and German professional associations are primarily study bodies: they are also consulted on educational and other matters but they do not work to control entry to occupations.

Essentially, Anglo-Saxon 'professional' management education has not been successful in training top business executives, because it was never really expected to. In the myth of management work, with its over-optimistic view of human motivation, it is assumed that the information provided by management scientists will make rational decision-making possible, even normal. Thus it is felt that individual programmes can be ranked in importance, tastes can be foreseen; and that the top executive can be portrayed as a decision-unit acting in a way which is broadly rational. So taught, management techniques have concentrated on decision-making; whereas reality shows that the top executive, in his largely unscripted part, is very much a different kind of actor from this description.

3 A culture of dependence

It has become clear that industrial or commercial performance cannot be thought about sensibly without reference to *culture*. It is pointless to make productivity comparisons with the Japanese, for example, unless you take into account the role of women and wives in Japanese society. To put it mildly, you could not get American women, for example, to put up with it. If the values of society decree that there must be relatively generous provision for public health, old age and so on, then the burden of costs upon industry will rise, and productivity, on a cost basis, will fall.

There is now a certain amount of agreement amongst social scientists and economists that Britain may be in some ways a laboratory for social forces at work elsewhere in the developed economies. In a new book, Bernard Nossiter of the *Washington Post* argues that Britain's peculiar situation, for all its multiple economic, political and social causes, must, in the end, reflect a kind of collective *decision*, albeit a subconscious one, to work less hard than before. This in turn may reflect a canny judgement, again in the subconscious, that the costs of a materialist culture probably outweigh its benefits, in the long run. It is certainly clear that the British have no real stomach for the new 'intermediate' institutions – that is the large bureaucracies of the modern economic order – precisely because you tend to lose your identity in them. A German or Japanese employee displays a degree of loyalty to the firm that would be inconceivable in Britain and positively alarming to the British. The Americans, I think, fall in between; Americans, especially 'managers' tend to be pretty loyal to the firm but can at least be got to laugh about it, with a bit of prodding (that must be the Anglo-Saxon strain in American blood and culture).

As I suggested before, the rural village is probably the preferred unit-size for the British – perhaps a few hundred to two to three thousand souls – big enough for requisite variety (and eccentricity) but not so big you lose touch with the edges. But that unit or village will be a reflection of the wider culture, a culture that has enjoyed relative stability over hundreds of years. Indeed, the country as a whole seems to be about as big as can be governed by the one legislature, without resort to federalism. In fact, the move to devolution in modern Britain may reflect in part the impossibility of making Welshmen and Scots feel that they have a realistic stake in Westminster government.

So, the wider culture is valued and cherished; people sense its very existence and longevity and feel a part of it; it is *there* as a symbolic backcloth to the tangible world of close and homely relationships in small units. There is a cost however; the British have paid virtually no attention to the development of constitutional structures and procedures for the new big industrial units. With industry shoved away unseen in the misty north and all big units despised in the first place, hardly anyone has paid attention to such things. No citizen in the world, in the role of *citizen*, has more individual liberty than the Briton, or better and more flexible recourse to justice and participation, because no other country has paid so much attention, for so long, to such things. But, conversely, few people in the developed world in the role of *employee* have been taken so much for granted.

The Germans, by contrast, have paid enormous attention to the constitutional aspects of work, employment and the rights and duties of employees. They have done so because, for a variety of historical reasons, Bismarck paid attention to such things at a time when 'Germany' as a nation was little more than a gleam in his eye.

I am not here arguing that one country is in some way 'better' than another – simply that countries *pay attention* to different things at different points of history, for perfectly logical reasons. It is not 'bad' that Britain has become a culture that reflects Dependent assumptions, any more than it is necessarily 'bad' that in recent history Germany, America and Japan have been cultures of Fight. In the first edition of this book, describing Britain as a culture of 'dependence' was seen as an attack by many people, and an attack from within by an ungrateful colonial. It is not meant to be an attack, but an *observation* born of respect and affection; where would we be without dependence; where would we be without mothers?

A German colleague once asked me what I took to be the most important British institution. Quick as a flash, I said, 'the pub' (which in many cases has supplanted the church as the glue that holds villages together) and, with a bit more thought, 'the Angry Brigade'. This motley collection of revolutionaries of the BA (Sociology) Honours (failed) type, will not be much known outside Britain, not, in any case, known in the way Baader-Meinhof is known. My German friend took the point; any country which throws up so witless and incompetent a challenge to the State has much to recommend it as a place to live and bring up children (whatever the tax system). The real revolution in Britain is against the intermediate institutions and it is pursued with fox-like cunning and Drake-like zeal.

Britain wasn't always dominated by dependent assumptions. For a very long time she could have been characterized as a culture of Fight – that is, whatever the internal order of things, at the external boundary the nation was engaged in highly aggressive trade, piracy and warfare and those who so 'represented' Britain were adventurers – the opposite of the dependent personality-type. By the twentieth century, whatever competitive and aggressive urges existed in the culture were not, it seems, being mobilized effectively at the national boundary in the same way – except, of course, for the world wars. Even here, the mobilization of Fight was a weary and reluctant process and substantial dependence upon the USA quickly, and inevitably, became a characteristic of the effort.

At some point, Britain had become predominantly a culture, of Dependence – a drawn-in, reflective, unambitious place, revering the female gods of existence rather than the masculine gods of action. Here I refer to the ideas of Wilfred Bion, the great genius of small group theory. Bion hypothesized that, beneath the level of rational, task performance, human beings in groups operate at any given time according to certain emotional patterns or basic assumptions. These 'basic assumptions' he described as Dependence, Fight/Flight and Pairing (a sophisticated variation of Dependence). Further, he suggested that aggregations of people, even (in the sway of powerful emotions) very large aggregations, may become gripped by these basic assumptions, or combinations of them, sometimes to the exclusion of rational, task-related behaviour – behaving *as if* their primary task was to depend utterly on a charismatic leader (Dependence) or to attack or flee from a more or less real bogey (Fight/Flight). That is not to argue that basic assumptions, because usually subconscious, are necessarily a bad thing; simply an inevitable, built-in part of the psychological make-up of humankind, a remnant, probably, of our more obviously primitive past. One cannot eradicate the basic assumption level of behaviour; one may, if one is alert to such things, be able to ensure that the prevailing basic assumptions are in reasonable harmony with *system* needs – either for internal sustenance or external coping with the environment.

In time of war, the mobilization of Fight/Flight, via adrenalin, will be directly task-related. To give examples; Hitler's mobilization of basic assumption Fight against the Jews clearly represented an expression of deep, pathological emotion which drove out rational thought in all save the minority. At the same time, it represented Flight from less palatable home truths. Equally, Chamberlain's reflection of basic assumption Flight (away from patently obvious realities) arose from a nation in a slumber of Dependence. In that particular setting, Churchill had to be defined as a troublemaker until, that is, the Fight became inevitable and the mobilization of a natural Fight leader became (rationally) task related. Without a Fight, Churchill was like a fish out of water; that was his natural valency, just as Chamberlain, as people sensed, was lost *in* one. Without Philip II as bogey what might have become of Drake? He would no doubt have ended up being investigated by the Elizabethan equivalent of a Director of Public Prosecutions.

What is the relevance of these ideas for industry and for management? The answer is that the mobilization of latent Fight/Flight behaviour is important in competition and therefore particularly in certain kinds of industrial roles. America, Germany and Japan are all cultures dominated to some extent by the Fight/Flight assumption, for a variety of historical reasons. Of these, only the *post*-Imperial powers have succeeded in diverting all their Fight away from war into international trade; the Americans, still perhaps in an imperial phase, have had communism as their consistently convincing bogey and as a result have stayed more or less consistently at war. The basic assumptions of Dependence and Fight/Flight will be present, just beneath the surface, in all kinds of activity, in shifting and unpredictable patterns. For any system to survive, whether it be an individual, a group, an institution, or even a country, it must provide sufficient support for the dependent needs of its parts, but at the same time, mobilize sufficient Fight (or perhaps Flight) to cope with emergencies at the boundary with the environment.

This is simply one way of representing the fundamental human dilemma – to huddle together with others, or with one's own existing assumptions, or to branch out, to risk, to cross over boundaries. We all need to do both, and the problems are those of choice and timing. To generalize, most of the managers I know, especially in big organizations, are much too timid, or apparently so. It would be better, on the whole, if they got out and made a few more mistakes, rather than saving up their complaints about what *can't* be done for the pub, or the bar, or wherever. The point is, they are not really timid at all; rather they cling to theories of the world which are conservative and dependent and which serve to justify over-cautious habits. This seems to me to be true for most big organization bureaucrats, but perhaps only in Britain is this tendency so reinforced by the culture.

After the war, it would have been realistic to regard Britain as engaged in a different kind of war, this time for world trade. Britain's more successful trade competitors defined their role in such terms and succeeded, over the years, in mobilizing effective 'fighters' at the national boundary to fulfil that role. By contrast, Britain, as a nation was purged of Basic Assumption Fight, and not surprisingly. Post-war legislation was primarily about providing a safety-net of care for all the people and eradicating the competitive Fight from key sectors of industry and bringing them under the wing of the State. I place no particular value on this, for the moment. The prevailing mood was hope and the prevailing assumption that the world, a large part of which still *seemed* to be under British sway, would return to pre-war 'normal'. The country was held in the mind as a 'good object' – successful in war and (apparently) prosperous and stable in peace. Under the surface, the structural and psychological problems remained as they had for a hundred years and more but there was still some capital to be used up, mostly American. The Basic Assumption of Fight did not disappear, because it doesn't, but was ingested rather than projected outwards. Underneath the calm, dependent surface, a pattern was developing of ritualized (binary) Fight between old adversaries – bosses and workers, north and south, Labour and Tory, left and right, rich and poor. Britain, as a whole, had become uncannily like the kind of family that becomes a casualty of a welfare state – dependent upon others, riven by habitual patterns of internal conflict, but stubbornly keeping alive an idealized, wildly inaccurate self-image.

In this context, nostalgia for World War II falls into place. So too does the half-wish for Armageddon, because, recent history teaches the British that only *in extremis* can Fight, at the national level, be summoned up. Within the culture, the locating of Basic Assumption Fight is difficult; industry ought logically to be seen as the natural repository for those of the population most inclined towards the Fight mode; it is the most obviously competitive area and it is undoubtedly thus elsewhere. But, in Britain, the real *social* Fight is to be *not* in industry; for many people, to be in industry at all is to have, so to speak, lost already. It might therefore be that many of the most competitive and aggressive elements in British society are to be found not in industry at all but in the professions, where their talents and drive are largely irrelevant to the balance of payments. Here, they are likely to fight successfully for the creation of a ludicrously inflated professional sector. As Illich has pointed out, the number of 'professionals' in parasitic occupations such as law and medicine governs the number of clients, rather than vice versa.

The doctors, for example, in both Britain and America, have succeeded in diverting colossal sums of money from potentially useful areas of medicine (from the point of view of the sick) into the bits that happen to interest them. They have fought as hard as, and probably dirtier than, most business executives would dare – and they have usually won. Some of the more indifferent doctors among them (from the Hippocratic angle) would make superb export sales executives. Probably, many of their fathers *were* in 'trade' (where the fight is) but managed to uplift their offspring socially into the most dependent trade of all, save possibly the Church. Once death, rather than sex, became the ultimate taboo, the doctors were bound to take over from the priesthood the ultimate dependence, and respectability.

Bion suggested that these underlying emotional patterns or 'basic assumptions' are always present in all human activities. 'Participation in basic assumption experience requires no training, experience or mental development. It is instantaneous, inevitable, instinctive.' The basic assumptions are phenomena of group life, but there may well be people, groups, institutions, and perhaps even nations, characteristically prone to recreate those situations which are dominated by one basic assumption or another. Some groups always behave, for example, as if one particular person could be relied upon to sort out all its problems (Dependence). That would be a pattern of *mature* Dependence if that person really were infallible; however, human beings being what they are, it is highly unlikely. If we take again the example of a deprived family, the unit as a whole may be totally dependent on the State and unable to fight effectively to improve its position in the environment. Typically, such a family will be riven by internal conflict (displaced from the environment) and prone to scapegoat one or another of its members, often with disastrous results. The middle-class family, by contrast, competes (i.e. mobilizes Fight) with great success in the environment for all manner of advantages, the most obvious being the breadwinner's fight for preferment and earnings. Inside, one is likely to find a dependent structure, within which children will learn to depend and, ultimately, to be dependable. That may not be healthy either, as there are plenty of middle-class parents who create immature *over*-dependence within and project all their aggression into work and other competitive arenas outside. If you happen to work for one of these, it can be no joke – the bastard at work who 'cuts off clean' at 5.30 p.m. and returns, all sweetness and light, to his adoring and admiring brood.

Let me take the idea of locating the basic assumptions a little further and look at the places where grown-up children go to work. The working-class adult's assumptions about work may be those of a family-like system based on internal conflict (and of external State support if you should happen to lose the fight); the issue is not whether, but whom, to fight. The natural adversaries, recognizable by their demeanour and exalted organizational roles cannot really understand what the fight is all about. Surely, they argue, the *real* fight is for orders versus the external competition and, to achieve this, we should *all pull together*. They might as well be talking different languages. If we then compare the British and German company structure, the British big company board, in a strange parody of Court, frequently contains a collection of otherwise harmless, but bemused peers of the realm who roll up to board meetings, ask one silly question to justify their fees and listen in bewilderment as the executive directors push through all manner of nefarious schemes. How can one possibly explain the presence of the non-executive peers except that they represent the bridge between the fell purposes of trade, on the one hand, and the Queen, on the other. The full board is therefore a pure expression of Dependence, in the sense that it helps to legitimize, to connect up the firm with society as a whole. Beneath that level, the fights break out, usually at the key discontinuities in the organizational structure – divisional directors, plant or branch managers, foremen, but most of all with the unions.

The German situation is complicated by the formal two-tier arrangement established with the help of the Americans after the war (actually, as I have pointed out, *émigré* Germans at one remove). There is some evidence to suggest that the upper board or executive committee (the *Vorstand*) is usually an altogether more coherent unit than the British full board and thus, in a variety of ways, can fight on behalf of the corporation with great effect (for one thing, the bankers almost invariably follow their money into board membership). If this is so, it would explain how, from the senior management level

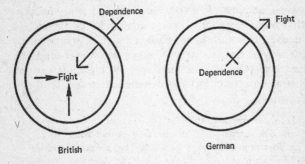

British   German

(lietende Angestellten) downwards, one tends to find a dependent structure – i.e. a structure within which managers know what they have to do and do as they are told – even foremen. For many Englishmen, such 'regimentation' is a proper object of xenophobic derision. All the multinationals have internal jokes about the impact of national stereotypes; one runs, 'When the orders come down from (somewhere in the USA), the Germans say they will do it and they do it, the Italians say they will do it, and they don't, the French never answer letters at all and the British argue and argue and end up doing half of it.' These little maxims always contain more than a grain of truth.

This sort of assumption about the relationship of Dependence to Fight has serious consequences. For example, few people would doubt that the calibre of the chief executive of any institution is crucial for its success. I have seen too many ailing organizations 'turned round' in an astonishingly short time, simply by replacing a dud with a really good man, to doubt the truth of this. But one eminent observer (Lord Wilfred Brown, himself managing director of a major engineering firm for many years and a Minister of State for Industry in the British Government, 1964-70) takes the view that 'about a third of Britain's manufacturing companies are in the hands of inadequate Chief Executives'. Lord Brown admits this is an intuitive view but it accords with my own experience and he has had a wider and subtler overview of company top managements than most government ministers.

Why then, we must ask, do not boards of directors, who have perfectly adequate authority for such things, divest themselves of the duds? (The right fight between the right people about the right issue at the right time.) Part of the answer might be that the board is held in the mind as a dependent structure; the fights are supposed to happen somewhere else. To quote Lord Brown:

External Directors very often know little more about the way in which the company is being operated than what they are told by the Managing Director at meetings of the Board. They are not, therefore, in a sound position to assess the effectiveness of the Managing Director. But, in many of our largest companies, the situation is worse than that. External Directors of such large companies tend to be drawn from very restricted strata of our society. Very often they have been personal friends of the Managing Director for years before being appointed. The Chairman, Managing Directors and external Directors of one company will meet each other in different roles on the Boards of other large companies. There is thus an 'incestuous' tendency which inhibits objective assessment in many cases. It takes rather more moral courage to cut short the career of an old friend than is possessed by most people.

Let me repeat that I am not *deploring* anything. Dependence and Fight/Flight are simply aspects of the human condition. It seems to me likely however that different cultures will express 'basic assumption' life in rather distinctive ways, whether the institution in question is a family, a school, a big commercial enterprise, or even the country itself. If British firms tend to establish a Dependent outside skin to the organization and to do most of the fighting inside (in-fighting), might this not reflect an image of the country as a whole, or even of family life? The average German or Swedish firm could be said to behave like a middle-class family (Fight at the boundary; mature Dependence within) and the less successful British firm like a troubled working-class one (Dependence on the boundary and Fight within). Could one then support the idea that the family, as an institution, has disintegrated to a greater extent in Britain than elsewhere; that in the working-classes in particular, it has been a major casualty of reduced circumstances? Whatever the divorce rate in Sweden, one can't help observing that, with the joint luxuries of wealth and space, the family as an idea seems to have a relatively good survival potentiality. I make the point because the family model is one of the structures which people at work carry over to try to make sense of their often bewilderingly large employing organizations.

The question is: what is valued; what can be depended upon? Is the institution of which one is a part sufficient unto itself, able to cope, or must there be some other Dependent object higher up, or further out? In this sense, the Church is the ultimate Dependent institution – because coming to terms with life and, more to the point, death means facing the inevitability of Dependence.

The relaxed manner of the British (unflappability) is attributed by Ralf Dahrendorf, the German sociologist and Director of the London School of Economics, to 'the fact that Britain is essentially at one with its history'. The existence of the English Channel helps to sustain this sense of boundary, continuity and of discreet withdrawal from the turbulent and revolutionary history of Europe. (The British feel, deep-down, about a Channel Tunnel the same way most housewives feel about mice boring into their kitchens. If it is *not* built, as I suspect, economics will get the blame but psychology ought to get the credit.) God, of course, resides to the west of the Channel.

In more frenetic cultures, the endless quest for 'growth' and material success are thinly-disguised evasions of (Fights against, Flights from) the inevitability of personal decline and death. Perhaps Britain is just now on the point of working through its own mid-life crisis, with Concorde as a last desperate night on the tiles. The Dependent state, thus, may help you to live more easily with the passage of time; to look age in the face and find the reflection benign. But the problematic side of Dependence arises in the 'intermediate institutions', the big dependent and dependable employers, because it is as dispiriting for employees of firms as it is for children in families to sense that those in charge cannot really cope with the challenge of the environment – that is, cannot Fight successfully on behalf of the institution. The main board *ought* to be dependable; an object of mature and critical Dependence. It cannot be if it ducks Fight.

I used the comparison of Germany above for the locating of Dependence and Fight in organizational behaviour. I am often asked: what about the French? The answer is, I don't really know. What are the 'basic assumptions' that dominate French culture and organization? Viewed as an economic contraption (by, for example, the Hudson Institute) the French economy, extrapolated, will grow faster than any other in Europe. But, for my money, the French, despite certain appearances, are more like the English than any other European culture, hence all the fighting and distrust over the centuries – an outcome of projective indentification, that is, hating your own awful bits when they turn up in others. Certainly, the chauvinism, élitism, anti-authoritarianism are all there, plus smugness, a crucial and somewhat useful element in the mix which has largely disappeared in Britain. For the sober Scandinavians and Germans, simple economic extrapolation probably makes sense, but the French could easily fall prey to internal fissures as deep and possibly more violent than those in Britain. The crucial difference, in recent history, is that the French, unlike the British, managed somehow to mobilze Basic Assumption Fight towards the Americans *after* the war. In a trade war, against daunting odds, that was an appropriate mobilization of basic assumptive emotion. 'La Défie Americaine' was, and had to be, written by a Frenchman.

The point of all this is that if British industry's ills are a function not of a failure to apply straightforward technical knowledge, but rather of deep underlying assumptions about behaviour, authority, work, role, legitimacy and integrity, then remedies will have to go correspondingly deep. I have grossly over-simplified the basic assumptions to make a point; in fact, all work will call on the mobilization of both Fight/ Flight and Dependence at different times, according to circumstance. In the 1970s, Britain needs to *fight* her way out of a corner, so that the mobilization of basic assumption Fight would make some sense; instead, there is a debilitating absence of adrenalin in the system; what Illich calls the 'paralysis of healthy responses to suffering'.

In America, the need is probably the opposite. Since Vietnam, a great many Americans have taken the view that commercial or military adventures in the outside world are less important than the state of the Union. To pursue Fights in the outside world, you need internal solidity and Dependence, or at least their appearance. Of course, one reason for looking abroad can be to paper over social cracks at home. Americans or other colonials who have chosen to live in Britain understand about the virtues (as opposed to the deficiencies)of a dependency culture, but they are also likely to feel (like Bernard Nossiter) that a *little* more Fight in the right places probably wouldn't turn Britain into a gun-toting, lawless jungle overnight. Americans sometimes wonder how the British have stayed so calm in the face of economic peril; anybody else would be in a state of near panic. But, in the Dependent condition, something will always turn up; God will provide. God *did*, in fact, provide – enough oil, out of the blue, to fuel the country for about thirty years – a miracle!

Nonetheless, there is a fight on and it is a fight for economic survival and all that that entails socially. It is almost as if the capacity to fight sensibly and constructively about things that really matter (like turfing out an inadequate chief executive, for example) has been forgotten or displaced into ritualized conflict (such as class warfare). Thus, it may become more important for the individual to keep his job (Dependence) than to take arms against the sea of lunacies which probably surrounds him at work. The useful Fight to hand is defined away elsewhere; it is *their* job (whoever they are); I am *not responsible*. If you are a professional, it is probably felt to be the fault of 'industry'; if a middle manager, the fault of 'the unions'; if a senior manager – 'the government'; if a trade unionist – 'management', etc. Either way, *something* has to happen, somewhere else, initiated by somebody else before anyone knuckles down to the fighting involved in putting right his own patch of responsibility. The final evidence of the dependent culture is provided by the posture of Government towards the people, with respect to the money-lenders – roughly paraphrased: 'Don't blame us, we don't want to hurt anybody, but what can we do? The IMF says we must tighten our belts.'

When the first edition of this book came out in late 1977, my colleague Professor John Morris pointed out that in focusing on the tension between Dependence and Fight/ Flight I had neglected Bion's third 'basic assumption' – Pairing. Pairing is, after all, a more hopeful assumption, less forbidding and unforgiving than the others. Bion, in his group studies, had observed that the Dependence of a group was frequently pressed upon not one but two people, almost as if by talking together interminably those two might conceive and bring forth some new infant who would lead the way to a more hopeful future. The essence of Bion's pairing argument, as I understand it, is not in the behaviour of the two, but in the voyeuristic and passive behaviour of the others.

John Morris was right – I was wrong to neglect creative pairing, especially with the recollection of Elizabeth I and Drake. But pairing for *work* is a different matter. Witness the remarkable pair of Russell Ackoff and Herman Wrice in the celebrated Mantua Project in Philadelphia in the late 1960s. Here, two men from wildly different backgrounds – a professor of Operations Research and a black from the Mantua ghetto (eight city blocks; population 22,000: 98% black) – worked together to create an urban rejuvenation programme that spawned, amongst other things, nine new manufacturing firms in the space of a couple of years, grossing $1.5 million and employing about 125 people from the community. The point of the story is that Ackoff grasped that white solutions to black problems hardly ever work and anyway 'we believed that blacks could learn more from their own failures than they could from white successes'. What this meant was that Ackoff and his colleagues from the worlds of university and fund administration had to learn to live with the uncertainties of handing over a major share of administrative and decision-making responsibility to the leaders of the black community, not versed in such things. That step depended in turn on a bond of trust that bridged the cultural line between the neat and orderly world of academia and the supermarket in which Wrice's wife was nearly killed in a shoot-out. Ackoff and Wrice forged that bond and it was the foundation of the whole project. But this was no passive, voyeuristic pairing, this was an uncomfortable, exposing partnership that pushed those all around into new and awkward areas of *work* – thus reducing the blacks' resourceless Dependence or mindless Fight and the academics' traditional Flight from the messiness of reality.

There are plentiful examples of creative, work-related pairing across boundaries. In Britain, the Wilfred Brown-Elliot Jaques (p. 88) pair led to one of the longest and most fruitful industrial/academic social science projects anywhere (the Glacier Project). Pairing is a romantic idea and the stories of pairs often have a romantic quality. Sir Arnold Weinstock, the head of Britain's highly successful GEC company, held out against the offerings of the 'management education' industry for many years, on the grounds that close attention to managerial responsibility, authority and example, and recognition of quality, seemed to 'develop' managers rather better than sitting in classrooms. Until the one night in living memory that Sir Arnold fell prey to illness and watched the T V instead of working: who should he see but Professor Reg Revans, the arch-iconoclast of management education, expounding (on the theme of Authority, decline thereof) – 'once a country starts to spend more on education than on beer, what do you expect?' Weinstock recognized a kindred spirit and, within the year, GEC's management development effort was entirely based on 'action-learning', Revans' design for helping managers to learn from their own messy experience. (I claim some small credit as midwife for all this, having scripted the programme and put Revans there in the first place.)

But, creative pairing aside, the great pair in Britain is the 'two sides of industry'. If there is something important to be done, don't establish those awkward characters with a fire in their belly who have strong opinions about how to do it; instead, select those who can 'represent' the 'point of view' of 'management' and then select an equal, or nearly equal, number of those who 'represent' the 'point of view' of 'the shop floor' (wherever it is) or 'the unions', or whatever. (There is a pool of committee-men skilled in this kind of 'representation'.) Then, having covered the territory, sit back, as passively as you like, as yet another committee grinds its way into oblivion, but working jolly hard at it all the while. *This* is Bionesque pairing, the hopeful belief, despite what your wits tell you, that this coming-together of the 'two sides' will be any different from all the others.

Let me end these musings on Dependence by returning to the matter of Fight. Universities don simply abhor mess, on our behalf, they are also pressed into the curious task of providing a sanctuary from the first significant Fight of adult life. My own recollection of university life is vague. But I *do* remember with gratitude being spared the necessity to grow up *quite yet*. For some of my contemporaries, who cracked the system, the sanctuary was permanent, like taking monastic orders. They have not emerged yet and they need not. The trouble is, some of them pronounce on matters of organization and management and, worse still, some of the managers actually listen to them. I have yet to hear a more convincing theory about the primary task of the university (postponement of Fight); students do seem to be prepared to put up with an awful lot from their tutors. But again, it is not a matter of 'good' or 'bad', but of timing. The prophet for our times was the late A. K. Rice (I think I quote him accurately): 'Fight is not a problem in itself; the problem is to ensure the fights occur between the right people, at the right time and about the right issues.'

The American connection

I have dwelt on the elements of Dependence and Fight/Flight, because they relate closely to the odd love/hate relationship, after the war, between Britain and the USA. To the observer of Britain the most striking feature of the post-war period is the poverty of imagination in relation to the new situation. Decisions were taken, as with the build-up of management education in the late 1950s and early 1960s, not because they seemed intrinsically right – to *fit* the circumstances – but rather because of a feeling that a fantasized disaster might follow unless *something* were done.

Absent leadership Dependence on the USA was massive, to the point where it is hardly an exaggeration to suggest that the leadership function in the collective mind of British industry was *vested* in America. This process, begun during the war, was carried on through the import of 'TWI' (Training Within Industry for Supervisors) based on group discussion methods. The 1951 Anglo-American productivity council team returned full of glowing and uncritical admiration of the American management education scene. There is no hint of a recognition that the American phenomenon had been constructed on an entirely different foundation with respect to cultural assumptions, natural resources and the characteristics of the labour force. These were the days when the 'special relationship' really seemed to mean something, when the British vision of America was built on an east-coast, British-oriented, Brooks Bros sub-culture. (The relationship *was* special for the dominant post-war Prime Ministers; the Churchills and the Macmillans had lots of American cousins.) But, middle-America (dominated, as it happened, by German immigration) was more Germanic in character – solid, thorough, Lutheran and not a little aggressive. In the European programmes of post-war reconstruction there was a natural affinity between German industry and its main tutor (see p. 24).

Meanwhile, Britain was soaking up some $2.7 billion in Marshall aid, against a mere $1.7 billion for Germany, a statistic, from Barnett, which demolishes a much cherished myth about the German economic miracle. In fact, in the post-war period, Britain received $8 billion in the form of direct grants or loans from a variety of sources. It isn't clear what happened to it all; certainly, by that time, the sterling area had become a liability and a lot of the Marshall aid money drained away through the exchanges. What the Germans got was spent in Germany. Dependence is a psychological phenomenon, an emotional patterning in collections of people, but it is always manifested in some concrete expression. The habit of borrowing beyond your means, a habit British governments have never lost since 1945, is a clear expression of the dependent assumption. With this example in front of us, we should not be surprised, having created a vast complex of segregated 'council estates' to find so many dependent families so deep in rent arrears. After the war, the Americans had the money, so that was where the money came from. There was a new fight in the offing – a war for world trade, but at the basic assumption level, Fight was spent.

The American influence did not stop at the level of productivity councils. British industrial practices were also powerfully influenced by American management consultancy: on the one hand, a small, but disproportionately influential band of management gurus, of which Professor Fred Herzberg was perhaps the archetype. British business, with its long and unlovely history of employee exploitation, fell with enthusiasm on American versions of 'motivation' – versions which promised the possibility of more effective ways of getting people to do things for you, together with a place in heaven for your good works. It was irresistible stuff. At the same time, the big consultancy firms were moving in and the fashion soon became established that one of them in particular had to be used in relation to the most hallowed British institutions: Government, the BBC, the Bank of England and so on. It was almost as if no one would really *believe* that a process of 'consultancy' (defined, in this manifestation, as drastic reorganization and the clearing out of dead wood – a kind of Augean cleansing) had actually occurred unless it were carried through by this firm and at enormous, painful, cost. No one ever expects this firm to *do* anything about its recommendations and scant attention is ever paid to the means by which ordinary people manage to subvert such plans, given a certain amount of time. The activity is symbolic; a purification ritual.

When the remarkable acceleration of management educational provisions took place in the 1950s and 1960s the American model was again, largely without criticism, accepted as gospel. The main protagonists of that growth now wryly admit that the American example may have been followed too slavishly but few can suggest convincing alternative ideas either. In some ways, the wish seems to have been to *have* a British Harvard Business School – that institution supposedly symbolizing the marriage of commerce and the traditional Ivy League universities. In Oxford and Cambridge, management and business had never really 'taken' even in the heady days following the Anglo-American productivity study team.

At the same time, the big American multinationals were steadily increasing their stake in British 'household name' firms. Their 'management development' practices began to cross the Atlantic soon after the war and to influence, to a greater or lesser extent, the personnel practices of British-owned firms. Thus, at many and significant levels of post-war industrial decision-making, Government, representation of major firms, consultancy and, increasingly, management education, the leadership was effectively provided by America. In a period when 'growth' for its own sake was accepted as a natural goal, nothing could have seemed more natural; but if the USA represented absent leadership in the mind (and sometimes in the flesh) what then was the nature of the present leadership?

Present leadership As I have said before, business and industry represent typically a natural catchment for the aggressive/

competitive component of the national subconscious. That is not to say that all businessmen are necessarily very aggressive, nor that the professional classes, the 'caring' professions or those in Government are devoid of competitive urges, but that the ends of industrial/commercial effort are goods and services which have to find buyers in a genuinely competitive market, if corporations are to survive. In industry, you have to believe in your products, not only as to price/quality competitiveness but as to intrinsic worth to the consumer as well, if you are to take up a legitimate competitive role at all. Only in large-scale industry is the solidarity/fighting posture of the military replicated so closely. After a war, where does the fight go in a dependency culture, tired of fighting? Clearly, much is channelled into all levels of business and industry, but most relevantly into industrial management; how many officers actually made the switch, or the return, in the post-war years cannot be said with accuracy. What can be said, in relation to current personnel, manpower and management development practices is that they have been powerfully influenced by the military, both as to underlying concepts of task, organization and leadership and in relation to specific practices and procedures.

The influence of the military in industry can be seen as the outcome of symbolic, ideological and practical considerations. The point of the post-war years was not so much having been in a war but having *won* a war. More than a generation later, nostalgia about that far-off victory runs higher than ever, if public taste is a reliable guide. To a nation still believing in economic growth as a primary aim, war-time victory stood out as the single peak in a long downhill slope to the economic second division. It is hardly surprising that an acceptable model of present leadership was automatically assumed to be military in character in many sectors of society, notably industry. The young veterans who came into industry in those years are only now approaching retirement, many of them at the highest levels; when they are all gone it does not necessarily follow that the solidarity picture of corporate life will vanish, so pervasive is the subculture of military ideology within the industrial management world – expression of internal conflict is not tolerated but projected outside or into traditional internal splits, or regulated by a variety of procedures – loyalty is prized above all else and rewarded disproportionately in relation to talent – career dependence (until recently anyway) is virtually absolute – the concept of leadership is conceived of charismatically and pays little regard to the complexities of managing and carrying authority for *systems* as opposed to networks of men. Moreover, at some level of the subconscious, ordinary people, and certainly ordinary soldiers, must be aware that the recourse to absolute solidarity and unquestioned 'authority' may not be unconnected with performance of an extremely difficult and intrinscially distasteful task – in the case of war, killing other human beings at risk of being killed oneself. It is a truism that industrial argot is full of such phrases as 'the front line', 'the sharp end' (which can be loosely translated as production management and selling).

In much of management thinking about management, war has dominated the scene . . . management development becomes rather like military training. Most of the language of business policy has been borrowed from the armed services. We talk of mobilizing a task force, getting the organization into action, corporate strategy. Managers consider morale and wonder whether they have dynamic leadership . . . none of this is surprising. Industrial and commerical activity in a capitalistic society is highly competitive and risky; harshness, self-sacrifice, comradeship, brutality all feature. Because of the enormous risks inherent in war the armed services have traditionally put a good deal of emphasis on training. Such training is by no means limited to relevant knowledge and technical skills; it is concerned with forming appropriate attitudes and values: tenacity, self-discipline, courage, determination, loyalty, fortitude. Many of these qualities are esteemed by managers. (Morris and Burgoyne, 1967.)

By the time the war ended, the military had learned, painfully and rather slowly, that leadership and followership had come a long way since Balaclava; whether post-war industry had absorbed the same lesson on any scale remained to be seen.

The essential challenge for British industry between the wars had been to forge new and workable roles for ownership, management and labour in relation to each other and to a consuming public. This was and had always been a complicated problem and certainly a problem which remained unresolved at the end of the war, and not only in Britain. The implicit assumption of a military model of leadership for running firms (as opposed to *changing* them) militated against grappling with such ambiguous and confusing issues. *Surely*, the team spirit which was so evident in war-time would simply carry over to a rejuvenated peacetime industry in a fairly straightforward way. An intriguing example of this kind of hope is provided by the important report 'Education for Management' put out in 1947 by a committee under the chairmanship of (who else?) Colonel Urwick. At the time, the management curricula of the British Colleges of Further Education no doubt needed some tidying up, but one cannot escape the impression that a tidying operation on this scale denied legitimate, even quirky differences of assumption as between disparate professions, industries and regions. The overriding assumption was that 'management' could satisfactorily be defined in the first place, then codified and taught just as such things had always been in the army.

The origins of the Henley Administration Staff College have this same flavour. Urwick himself had written an article in 1944 advocating the establishment of a national industrial staff college. He had also given to the first Principal the idea of encouraging students to study the careers of great men – Wellington, Cromwell, Peel etc. – in order to learn by example. Noel Hall (writing in 1949) said, 'Among the factors that weighed with me when the question of my going to the Administrative Staff College was under consideration was my good fortune in war-time of working at very close quarters, in the first eighteen months of the recent war, with a number of those who had passed through the Services Staff College.' Henley was thus, apart from anything else, an embodiment of nostalgia. It was, however, as British in conception as its later competitors were to be American.

The practical virtues of the military approach to corporate manpower matters are obvious if the increased size of post-war organizations is taken into account. Natural growth and the acceleration of mergers and acquisitions meant that British industry, for the first time, contained a substantial number of really large corporations; hence the new need to 'keep tabs on' an increasing number of people – who and where they were, how were they classified as to task, rank, pay, etc.; how well did they perform, might they be posted elsewhere? And so on. This is, of course, the dependency aspect of military organization – modelled on an organization which clothes, houses, feeds and indoctrinates its own in order to reinforce the sense of total membership assumed necessary for task performance. That task, increasingly, became a 'peace-keeping role' in military recruitment advertising. In recent years, British army promotional advertising for short-service commissions has oft-repeated a full-page newspaper advertisement almost completely filled with the signatures of general and personnel managers of major corporations, underwriting the thesis that three years in the army is at least as good a preparation for industrial management as a similar period in a university. This enterprise is rich in meaning; firstly, it is a massive reinforcement of one aspect of binary thought, the 'practical man' thesis, as against the 'intellectual'. Secondly, its appeal is universal: no doubt a man who *has* had the experience of getting a tank out of a river is better equipped for crisis management than a graduate in arts, but he can also be relied upon to get his hair cut when told. The two are inextricable.

Wounding and healing in a culture of Dependence It is perhaps a paradox that the acceptance of a military model in industry might have been a reinforcement of Dependence rather than Fight/Flight and that ideas about ruthlessness, radical change, aggression and drive were somehow projected into a fantasized American-style leadership. In consultancy, for example, the two post-war archetypes are a cool young hatchet-man doing an American-style 'reorganization' and, on the other hand, a somewhat older British ex-officer called in to help with 'human relations problems', 'communications' and the like. It was as if the taking of hard decisions was inevitably so painful a process that it could not be owned; what *could* be owned was the task of healing the wounds presumed to follow inevitably in the wake of such decisions. These were the respected skills of a feminine, care-dominated culture, the 'Mother Country' not the 'Father-land'. The process was one of progressively giving over the authority (to an absent form of leadership) to take the kinds of painful decisions which had become inevitable in post-war British industry – a role not unlike that of the itinerant hangman in the American Wild West. A par-

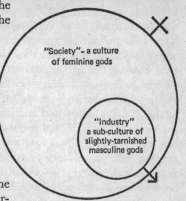

"Society" - a culture of feminine gods

"Industry" a sub-culture of slightly-tarnished masculine gods

tial exception may be the computer industry where painful decisions may be passed to the hardware suppliers and the work actually done by systems designers so young that they cannot comprehend (yet) the full (human) consequences of the changes they wreak. Somehow, the career dynamics of the computer world contrive to ensure that the young systems designers at the interface are always kicked upstairs at about the point they threaten to approach maturity.

However, in a culture of Dependence, the creative arts (celebrations of being, rather than of getting or having) may flourish. An American, talking of the 'legitimate theatre' has Shakespeare and Olivier in mind. Even the heartland of American pop music (not the pap) is substantially British (the original Tin Pan Alley was in London, not New York). British publishing is underpaid, but immensely prestigious – probably the only respectable 'trade' to be in where there is actually a manufactured object (as opposed to merchant banking for example; though how anybody can regard that as a respectable trade is mystifying); what's more, the object is valued for its own sake. But if you happen to be in business to make almost anything else, that really is 'trade', and regarded as not calling for insight, good design, aesthetic values or any real devotion to quality and care. Unless, that is, you happen to work for foreigners. Some rational explanation has to be found for the disproportionate success of foreign-based multinational firms operating in Britain with British staff. Either there is something quite distinctive about the foreign style and practices which liberates something special in British employees and/or there is some special population of Britons drawn to the foreign-based multinational in the first place. My subjective impression, gained from intermittent 'soft' research (i.e., conversations in pubs) is that the workers of foreign-based multinationals are likely to say four things: 1 They keep you up to it. 2 They work you hard. 3 They look after you. 4 They pay well. In other words, foreign-based multinationals tend to have a certain local repute which has to do with the maintenance of certain *standards*, both on the part of employers and employees. The evidence is, it works.

On this issue of standards, let me reproduce two revealing quotes, from a senior executive of two of the biggest Swedish firms, about their British operations:

Why don't they keep the factory clean?
Once they have got it that they *have* to do it, it is all right!

The trick, for the Swedes, appears to rest in treating Britons *as if* they were Swedes; as if their attitudes to work and employment were untainted by 200 years of British industrial history. After a time, it seems that British workers begin to *behave* a little like Swedes, regarding Swedish standards as acceptable and normal rather than excessive. This the phenomenon of Absent Leadership in a clearcut form and it may be an important example because, in the minds of the British, the Swedes are not, in my experience, associated with ruthless efficiency and monolithic bigness in the same way as the Americans are. It may therefore be that, if the British *must* accept Absent Leadership, the Swedish example may be a more sympathetic and hence useful model for us than the American.

Interestingly, British observers of the successful foreign firm seem to me to misunderstand the phenomenon. The Sony company of Japan, for example, has been as successful in South

Wales as in America. I carried out a study for the Department of Industry in the UK which concluded, amongst other blindingly obvious things, that Sony and other foreign firms got good productivity because British workers (any workers for that matter) actually *liked* working hard, to high standards for people who care passionately about quality. They also like it with British managers provided they can find some who feel good about what they are doing in the industrial subculture instead of looking on it as an escape ticket to respectability.

The BBC did a revealing TV programme about Sony in South Wales They. referred to the early morning *work* meetings (about schedules, sales figures and design modifications) as 'pep-talks'. The awarding of prizes for good timekeeping was described, with a xenophobic smirk, as 'the carrot end of a subtle Oriental blend of stick-and-carrot.' The media, and many of the behavioural scientists too, have fallen into the trap of assuming that if high motivation is present, somebody must have been 'motivated' by somebody else. Of course, TV producers and behavioural scientists take a pride in their *work*; get their motivation from *it*. However, some of them find it a little hard to believe ordinary workers might do the same. Some of the foreign firms have demonstrated that the world is not split into good (gentle, fair, dependent) bits and bad (tough, unfair, aggressive) bits. The good institution, and the good boss, is 'tough but fair' and gives a damn about what it or he is doing.

Thus, the post-war period can be seen as having the same *split* character as the inter-war years. On the one hand an *actual* acceptance of a model of management which seemed to have worked well enough over five years of war and which fulfilled in many ways a deep-seated wish for a return to a simple dependent world; on the other hand a notion of aggressive management-in-the-mind which was in some ways antipathetic to the post-war culture but was at the same time seen as necessary medicine for the chronic ills of British industry. Of course, the essential, messy problem was to work at the task of *integrating* the needs of a dependent culture with the realities of a completely changed world, to be able to cope with the taking of painful decisions in a realistic way – in other words – to fight. As things worked out, the 'two cultures' of industry (absent and present – American and military – tough and caring) operated in a kind of independent disintegrated harmony. Many would argue that the turbulent political climate of the post-war years indicates important changes in national assumptions, but the move from Utopian, rebuilding ideas to the more *laissez-faire* fifties, and the switch to Tory government in 1951, perhaps ought to be seen as a drift from one deeply dependent set of assumptions to another: from 'We will nationalize it on your behalf' to 'You've never had it so good'.

By the late fifties, management development and management education were about to become the big growth industries. When one comes to consider the acceptance, or otherwise, in the UK of an American phenomenon such as 'management development', such cultural matters are paramount. Management development is a solidarity concept, a concept which keeps alive the assumption that all may enter the halls of management and all may rise within them. The Fight/Flight culture, whether it be a nation or an enterprise, achieves internal solidarity by projecting Fight outwards. But, after the war, Britain completed the process of giving away an empire; her great industrial enterprises, with notable exceptions, neglected exports to satisfy the booming home market and, militarily, the Suez fiasco rounded off the process of 'coming home'. At the same time, and over many years, the Colonial administrators had been coming home, bringing with them firmly entrenched benevolent/xenophobic attitudes about subject races which could only spell long-term trouble in post-war British industry. The essential change for Britain was the reingestion of Fight/Flight within the national boundary, the reinforcement of the traditional bi-polar splits of opinion between left and right, them and us, north and south and so on – a Flight from the middle ground. The same thing held true for enterprises; one of the sociologist's favourite questions for international comparison is, 'If business were a football match, do you see yourself on the same, or a different side to management?' Workers in Britain, almost uniquely in Europe, see themselves as on the opposite side of the pitch.

4 The post-war managers

7 The manager as technocrat

(*The 'professional' Mk. II*) My seventh manifestation of the manager derives from an historical oddity – the so-called 'managerial revolution' which began life as a book by that name in 1942. The author was James Burnham, an American, later to be a favourite of the National Front pamphleteers and speech-writer for George Wallace. His thesis was a simple anti-Marxist one: 'The falsity of the belief that socialism is about to arrive has been shown by an analysis of the unjustified assumptions upon which that belief is usually based and by a review of specific evidence countering that belief.' Instead, he argued that, 'We are now in a period of social transition in the sense which has been explained, a period characterized by an unusually rapid rate of change of the most important economic, social, political and cultural institutions of society.' This transition is from the type of society which we have called capitalist or *bourgeois* to a type of society we have called 'managerial'.

After the fashion of Bishop Ussher, Burnham dated the process as beginning in 1914 and finishing in 1964. A one-time Trotskyite, Burnham saw the growth in state ownership of the major instruments of production as leading inevitably to the creation of a managerial élite based on control rather than a (capitalist) stake in the action. Burnham's predictions look a little sorry with hindsight, including his guess at a German war victory, but the important point about him is the influence of his thesis on both sides of the Atlantic at least until the mid-1960s. Above all, it was an *attractive*, egalitarian, middle-ground thesis which threatened no one save the despised owners, and offered much by way of ushering in a new order based on free competition, competence based on education rather than social position and so on.

In the late 1950s, while a collection of (largely) Tory ministers and businessmen were hatching the new business schools, and management education was finding its way into the manifestos of both Parties, the thinking wing of the Labour Party, in the form of the late Anthony Crosland, was also taking up the managerial revolution theme. His paper 'The Future of Socialism' in 1959 echoed Burnham in most respects: British capitalism had entered a state of non-crisis and stability, the State had already aggregated a significant part of the power of the business-class, full employment had led to a significant increase in the bargaining power of labour and, above all, there had been a significant devolution of power from top executives to 'specialists', rewarded by salary rather than a profit share. In such conditions, he argued, the old idea of class politics was less relevant – 'Private industry is at last becoming humanized'; and, as to labour disputes – 'The angry clamour of past struggles is now heavily muffled.' Crosland was wrong about much of it, it happens, but in the process he helped pave the way for an election victory based on the notion of technological 'white heat' and the sweeping away, perhaps in the wake of Suez, of the old, the privileged and the complacent. It was a return of the renaissance thinking of the immediate post-war years, but this time with the *manager* centre stage. This must have represented the high point of belief in 'technical' management; the matter of legitimization could be expected to take care of itself within this new aristocracy.

With hindsight, it is difficult to distinguish this newly packaged technocrat manager from the original 'professional' manager of the 1920s. His appeal was precisely the same; he would somehow hold the middle ground between the entrenched positions of the vested interests (more of them now and on the whole less controllable than the old family owners) and labour, and he would do it through education and technical excellence. If anything, he was to be a little less like the 'professional' of the old professions and a little more like a professional footballer – a 'real pro'. Increasingly, the pro footballers started to make a lot of money and to behave like thugs – which is where we came in (in 1579). At any rate, everybody, or almost everybody, bought the product the second time round and the honeymoon lasted about ten years; until, in fact, it became clear that a significant proportion of the growing numbers of unemployed were these same 'professional' managers.

8 The constitutionalists

After the war, something important was happening at the Glacier Metal Company in Britain. The Glacier story is well-known to students of management the world over, probably better known on the Continent of Europe than in Britain. I referred (p. 73) to the crucial partnership which developed between Wilfred Brown (the managing director until 1964; now Lord Brown) and Doctor Elliot Jaques, the (then) Tavistock Institute social scientist who acted as independent analyst of the company's operations over a generation. That partnership was built on a recognition of the importance of psychological insight into organizational affairs. For example, Jaques and Brown were pretty clear that there is usually a difference between (i) formal statements of aims, (ii) what people *think* they are doing and (iii) what they may be observed by others to be up to. Furthermore, all these may differ from (4) *requisite* or optimal performance; hence the importance of independent analysis.

The historical importance of the Glacier experiment is not to be found in what has been done (though that is important) but in how what has been done is misunderstood and misrepresented by others. At base, Glacier has been built on the idea that people at work are entitled to (and likely to respond to) the same kinds of constitutional rights as they have come to expect in the role of citizen. The company therefore has to elaborate those arrangements – that is, write them down so everybody will know exactly what they are, and then devote a considerable proportion of its time to modifying them in the light of a continuous social/technical analysis, and an analysis of some subtlety, as I have indicated above. That is not *all* the company has to do; as Wilfred Brown points out, Glacier has been a successful company because it has designed and made plane-bearings and supplied them (on time) more effectively than most of its competitors.

What then have the others, principally the organizational/behavioural scientists, government functionaries and other executives, made of it? The answer is, I think, revealing and could be summed up thus:

1 It is new (probably new-fangled).
2 It is fussy (probably a lot of red tape and endless meetings).
3 It is a bit pinko (Brown is a Scotsman and was a Socialist peer to boot).
4 It is do-goodism (probably 'industrial democracy' gone mad).

There are echoes of Francis Drake in this response. He was in a very old trade indeed, in which you took decisions fast and asked questions afterwards; if you stopped to consider the morality of it all, you would lose profits to competitors. Of these responses, I think the last is the most powerful, as though Glacier were a re-emergence of Quaker morality into the naughty world of Lockheed and Slater-Walker. In the tough world of big business (where the real men are) your strength, it is assumed, will be sapped by such effete considerations from the caring and reflective mother culture. But the Quakers were great constitutionalists too.

The truth about Glacier is that:

1 It is not essentially new; it has always been an entirely conventional company structure;
2 There *are* a lot of meetings at Glacier and a good deal of writing-down, but all of it is necessary. It is a fallacy, beloved of Englishmen, that the British Constitution is not a written one; it simply happens to be written down in different places

in different forms, but it is watertight just the same, and responsive. It would *never* have taken the British all of three years to get rid of Richard Nixon.

I referred earlier to the Sony Company of Japan. Let me quote one Welsh worker there (on the Japanese): 'They pay almost *pedantic* attention to detail; things take a long time to get right – but they *do* get them *right* in the end!' It is a crucial skill in managers, in my view, to be able to tell the difference between real bureaucratic red tape and those things you simply *must* get right, in detail, at length.

3 Is do-goodism the same as enlightened self-interest? I think not. It is not difficult to observe the lessons of history and to see that the constitutional arrangements Britain has enjoyed for hundreds of years have, for the most part, *worked*. The blind spot is to imagine that such arrangements have no place in work organizations. But if industry is seen as a split-off, aberrant, aggressive, amoral subculture of society, then naturally it will hardly be worthwhile trying to civilize (or constitutionalize) it. Instead, the sensible thing is to 'do time' in industry and stock up (like a squirrel in summer) for a retreat to 'the good life'. I am afraid the same splitting can be found in American business life; American businessmen are much more likely than their European counterparts to take their consciences to church with them on Sundays. England is full of churches surrounded by non-attending, commuting executives who yell blue murder if the Church threatens to pull down a redundant building. The importance of the church, in the fabric of an idealized community, is that it is *there* to be stayed away from.

The truth is, Glacier is too close to home; the example is too obvious, too straightforward, too damned easy to replicate, with a bit of effort (I don't imagine the company to be perfect by any means). Better for the weak of spirit to condemn it as trendy, laborious or wishy-washy. (I have ignored the 'pinko' nonsense, on the grounds that some readers don't require comment on it and those that do are past redemption.) Perhaps the best illustration of the Glacier principle comes from elsewhere – from Germany. An important study of the two-tier board arrangements there concluded that, when formally-constituted board meetings occur, most of the important decisions have been taken already – between the distribution of the agenda and the meeting itself. As the works council and other key interests are party to this pre-work, the main board rarely demurs. The German response, a variation of 'if it moves, salute it!' was 'if it works, institutionalize it!' The Anglo-Saxon response might, I suspect, be 'Great! The lads are working it – we don't need all that red tape!'

The underlying fallacy is that structures are equivalent to straitjackets; that the Anglo-Saxon's precious 'freedom' will be throttled by structure. The truth is, and anyone with young children can observe it, that real freedom grows out of shape and form and certainty. Adults, as well as children, need to know what the rules are in order to be truly free; to cross a boundary, you need to be fairly sure where it is. I always find, on lecture platforms, that when I talk of 'shape, form, structure', someone will come back to accuse me of arguing for 'discipline, control, authoritarianism'. Many people, it seems, cannot see the difference – it says a great deal about their parents or the schools they went to.

The true significance of Glacier is that, although it is on all the library shelves and in all the management curricula, its impact on management generally has been almost nil. It has been split off from the mainstream, just as the hard-headed Quaker firms were a hundred years ago.

9 The manager as scapegoat

Finally, after Burnham's managerial revolution had gone the way of all the others, the manager was left with what? Increasingly, it began to look as if 'management' (that is industrial Management III) was being held accountable by society as a whole for society's endemic ills. The ultimate manifestation of the dependency culture was the assumption that the primary task of management was no longer simply to run things properly, but to maintain full employment in an overblown, overproducing, overconsuming world. Alternatively, the primary task of Government was no longer, either, to run things properly, to do what is likely to *work*, but, likewise, to maintain full employment. The manager could increasingly be assured that if the firm went bust, Government might well step in to maintain employment directly, at vast cost to other taxpayers somewhere else. If these are the central assumptions of a culture, enshrined in the democratic process, then the model of change, of being cruel to be kind, of caring for the task first then the people, has to come from elsewhere; probably America still. If the managers cannot be entrusted with these tasks then they will be blamed in the end, wheresoever the blame belongs. By the beginning of the 1970s, management was beginning to wear a harried and crestfallen air. Far from being a homogeneous élite they were in increasingly fierce competition with each other for a reducing number of 'Mickey Mouse' jobs.

How can one support the idea of the industrial manager as scapegoat in Britain? What has happened to managers in the last few years? In the first place, managers have seen a remarkable erosion of their take-home pay, relative to almost all other callings. It hurts at two levels, in the wallet directly because, amongst other things, the (obligatory) private school fees are rising faster than post-tax income and it hurts also because it symbolizes a revised evaluation of the manager in society. Five years ago the manager could brood about social acceptance all the way to the bank; now society's verdict has become inescapable. Secondly, and reflecting this new valuation, more executives are out of work now than at any time since the war. The true figures are a matter for debate because managers, characteristically, are coy about incorporating themselves in such statistics. Informed observers have no doubt that the 'shake-out' is far from over yet and that many thousands of managers must be living in the shadow of redundancy – i.e. the death of their own careers. A few years back, it was largely unthinkable that the biggest corporations might *themselves* die. It is no longer unthinkable and to the extent that managers become incorporated in their organizations, as though they were one flesh, so may they be shocked by this new demonstration of the fragility of their world.

Now, if organizations find themselves (by 'themselves' I mean the main coalitions of influence at the top of them) able to divest themselves of so many managers, it must say something about staffing levels in management. If one of the main unstated tasks for an industrial employee is to rise from the ranks, then it follows that, in order to sustain a workable sociotechnical system, in the fat years there will be long hierarchical chains of management, short spans of control and a great many 'management' posts with, to say the least, ambiguous responsibilities of a management kind, however that word is defined. In lean times, you shed fat all over the body corporate and, as any dieting woman knows, it often comes off first in the wrong places. A similar process has been going on, during the 1970s, in the USA too; recent research indicates that, in the traditional home of the aggressive manager, there is a much increased concern with job security and a quick growth in preparedness to be represented by union-like organizations. US evidence also suggests that managers are increasingly turning down opportunities for promotion in order to pursue quieter, less risky lives. In the UK there has been a dramatic increase in membership of white-collar unions and the British Institute of Management, the official representative body for managers, is coming under increasing pressure to behave in a union-like way although, of course, stopping short of actually becoming one (Heaven forfend).

This is bound to be a tricky and uncomfortable balancing act, straddling, as it must, the respectability line of British binary thought. What the middle and junior managers want is to continue to pretend that they are more than mere agents, but to hold in reserve the despised strength of a union-like affiliation. They are not yet ready to fight their bosses, if they ever could be, but 'government' is an acceptable bogey and the wish, understandable in a dependency culture, is to have a 'voice' at the centre of society, and especially with the government, in the same way as representatives of the employers and the trade unions. It is a depressing prospect, because it may have little to do with the instrinsic *authority* of roles in the middle and much to do with trying to steal, or borrow, a little *power* from both extremes instead of just one. It may be, in other words, an expression of dependence (catching daddy's eye) rather than a *Fight* for a properly authoritative role in society.

5 A word for the product

(a word for production, lumpy objects and sex)

Evelyn Waugh, while registering satisfaction that he belonged to an ennobled family, bemoaned the fact that his forebears had been elevated for doing something useful. Far better, he said, to be of the other sort, where 'nobility' is given, irrespective of effort. In this, Waugh captured well the latter-day British attitude to manufacture. I have discussed at length the legitimatory function of the so-called management movement – that is, the process by which management came to mean *being* something or other rather than *doing* something or other. The simple-minded observer of the scene must ask why the end products of industry do not support legitimacy on their own. A single craftsman's legitimacy derives from his craft; so too do his profits in the long run. Why should the British, almost uniquely in Europe, seek legitimation of manufacture in the creation of an illusory brotherhood of people with, across the whole spectrum, not much in common except their social status?

The myth of the generalist One obvious answer (not, of course, peculiar to Britain) is the increasing size of organizations. Clearly, the more removed you are from consumers on the one hand and those who actually make products on the other, the more likely it is that the process of management may seem to have nothing to do with either. But unique to Britain seems to be the implicit belief that, having crossed over, you can't look back, as though the boundary to the portals of management was the River Styx itself. The people who understand the business *best* (though in a fragmented way) are salesmen and shop floor operatives because they actually handle the thing, whatever it is, in relation to unforgiving physics and an equally unforgiving market. Those jobs, as we know, are ones you are supposed to *rise* from if you want to be respectable; Waugh understood; they are too *useful*.

At this point, we collide with another prime example of binary thought – the ludicrous splitting of 'generalists' from 'specialists' as though they were mutually exclusive. In my own time in industry I reckon myself to have had only two really outstanding bosses. Both were men with a feel for the broad picture *together with* a feel for the particular – breadth of vision *plus* a meticulous eye for detail. That, in my terms, is the true 'all-round man' – someone with a concern for standards as well as a philosophy. In fact, a generalist, in the usual British sense, is really no more than another, and more rarefied, kind of specialist. I commented earlier on the disproportionate success of foreign-based multinationals in Britain versus indigenous companies. I suspect it has much to do with foreigners' disinclination to draw the distinction so clearly and so exclusively. A top Swedish engineering manager put it succinctly to me: 'If I go down on the line, it is because I want to see if the fix on yesterday's production worked; an Englishman probably goes down because they told him on a course that the workers like it. They can tell the difference!'

Games people play A further outcome of bigness is the creation of a competitive ball park in middle management where the rules of the game and the criteria of performance are so vague that the players tend to deal in power rather than authority. The fundamental authority of a manager relates, at one level or another, to the end products of the enterprise as a whole, but his *power* has only to do with his competitive position in the local jungle. Those with a win/lose mentality (perhaps a tendency towards Fight/Flight) may be drawn into a 'zero-sum' game which has little or nothing to do with the enterprise's essential purposes and everything to do with trying to gain an advantage in an ill-defined and sometimes dirty competition.

The American psychoanalyst Michael Maccoby has coined the term 'game character' to describe that blend of meticulously controlled aggression, flexibility, detachment, coolness under stress, aptitude for team work, the ability to see and feel in competitive terms and to experience the continued urge to *win* which characterizes American executive success. One way of viewing game character is as a highly successful psychological strategy in a situation where reality lies some distance from work: 'The game character is happiest when his work is most like (competitive) play.' Maccoby, in the great tradition of the guru behavioural scientists he deplores (such as McGregor and Maslow) has managed to sell a lot of books to American executives who like a little flagellation, but not too much. The distinction between 'gamesman' and 'jungle fighter' would probably be lost on a European (especially one who has stared Nazism in the face) but is highly palatable to those jungle fighters who still go to church every Sunday. In fact, behavioural science itself has become more a game than a craft.

Arguably, British management has more phoney generalists, but fewer game characters than the Americans – a natural outcome of a dependent, snobbish and non-competitive culture, as opposed to a Fight-dominated, egalitarian one. However, the essential clerkishness of the British psychology is well-suited to a more muted form of combat – on paper. Whilst American power politics may be played out in the flesh, conflict being an acceptable phenomenon in a Fight/Flight culture, in Britain, a dependency culture, Fight is likely to be displaced into salvoes of paper. It can be just as deadly; if verbal abuse is a bomb, a cunningly constructed memorandum has to be thought of as germ warfare. The problem is that it diffuses the important issues even further; you may sense that you are involved in some kind of fight but it may be difficult to know with whom and about what. In the dense middle management bureaucracy, the fight, or the game, is unlikely to have much to do with making artefacts and selling them.

Dominant throughputs, constraints and lumpy objects Another respect in which British organizations may be distinguished from those on the Continent is the number of accountants occupying seats in boardrooms up and down the country. Let me be quite clear, I have nothing in particular against accountants; some of my best friends are accountants, although it doesn't follow I want my daughter to marry one. There are simply too many accountants in high places in British industry and business and their preponderance says something about a collective perception of industry in general and manufacturing in particular. It is as if the primary task of industry was laundering money, with production as an irksome constraint on that primary task rather than vice versa. Again, this is hardly surprising in a nation built on a foundation of greed, where the surviving genius is to be found in those institutions where money, rather than artefacts, *is* the dominant throughput.

My theme here is that one kind of person dreams up and designs a product, another kind makes it and another again takes it out on the road to sell it. Even insurance salesmen, for example, have a capacity to think in almost physical terms about the product, and rightly so. This is, in other words, the dominant throughput process of a manufacturing enterprise:

---

raw materials/components
first conversion process (manufacture)
finished goods
second conversion process (transfer of ownership – i.e. sale)
generation of revenue
purchase of more raw materials/components etc.
survival

Everybody else, the accountants, the personnel folk, the head office specialists, are peripheral to this central process, even the management types who raise cash out in the environment; you cannot do it without a stable manufacturing and sales base.

We tend to accept that people from different specialisms think differently, but I doubt we realize *how* differently. How *do* you get inside the mind of another, to see how he constructs his world? It can't be done, of course, except by observing his behaviour and *inferring* from that – that he appears to believe he inhabits a world with such and such characteristics, quite different from one's own. The alternative is to pronounce him a bit queer and not, if one has that authority, to promote him. The main differences seem to me to occur between those in clerkish callings (that is, those who deal primarily in the symbolic world of words and figures expressed, when it matters, on paper) and those (let me call them converters) who, from time to time, come into smart contact with lumpy objects (that is, those who design, make, sell and install artefacts). The test that converters are engaged in the dominant process of manufacturing industry is supplied by the fact that if they do *not* successfully carry through the conversion task allotted to them (it is always accurately measurable) they do not and cannot survive, no more than their employing organization can.

I am indebted to a British civil servant (characteristically, a one-time converter now confined to clerkish activity) for the concept of the 'Robinson' as a unit of measurement – that is, the equivalent (90 kg) of the bulkiest and heaviest movable object a clerkish person ever has to contend with in work or play – as it happens, Robinson, down the corridor; even Mrs Robinson is unlikely to top 60 kg. People in clerkish roles (doubtless with a life-long clerkish predilection) do not have any experience of, and cannot therefore properly comprehend, the three-dimensional world of bulk, lumpiness, weight and unpredictability which lies outside their immediate purview. I speak with feeling, having more than once had to reassemble the pieces of human beings who had come off second best in encounters with more substantial matter than themselves. The experience teaches, amongst other things, a profound respect for the physical properties of matter, especially in large, wobbly, or liable-to-explode arrangements. I can describe these experiences and my feelings about them but I cannot put their peculiar quality into a clerkish person. If I could, I could probably make him a better 'manager' overnight; more humble, to begin with, and less likely to place unquestioned reliance upon structured techniques of 'decision-making'. If there were two ingredients I most wanted to inject into clerkish veins, they would be inspiration and panic.

In most big organizations a disproportionate number of top people are clerkish because they were selected and promoted by an earlier generation of their own ilk. They are not wilfully keeping out those people who understand the nether world of lumpy objects and blood and guts; they simply do not understand them and the world they represent, any more than if they were Trobriand Islanders. In small organizations, and especially manufacturing ones, there *is* a certain earthiness in high places, but no one has bothered much to carry the undoubted benefits of sophisticated management education to them. Why bother? – the big company clerks keep coming back for more.

It is plausible therefore to suggest that the cinderella of British industry is production management itself. After the war, it was said that Britain's real weakness was in *marketing* (whatever *that* means) and that she was too 'production oriented'. It may have been true in parts of industry, but the overwhelming picture from at least fifty years *before* was of weaknesses in production together with a complacent resting on the laurels of the Victorians, particularly the Scottish engineers who constructed many of the great machines of the industrial revolution. Indeed, one can say that the British have performed *prodigies* of salesmanship in continuing to shift poorly designed and over-priced products in increasingly fierce international markets. Arguably, the British genius, aside from money, *is* marketing.

Indeed, one can argue that the word marketing *means* quite different things in different cultures. It is, like so many other 'management' words, an English-language export via America and it certainly sounds grander and possibly more respectable than selling. It is also, as 'management' is an example of 'nouning', a good example of verbing – the German/American habit of activating nouns. The British, with a *genius* for advertising, take marketing to mean the creation of favourable impressions about probably indifferent artefacts. To a Swede, for example, marketing is more like telling it like it is (and attending meticulously to every little detail till the customer has it working). Telling it like it is works so long as the product can be relied upon to sell itself in the end. With such marketing skills, marginal improvement in British design and production would work wonders. Why has production slipped so in Britain? I can think of no explanation so convincing as that production is associated, in the national subconscious, with factories, and factories with satanism.

Integrity a product of the product The matter of production management is not simply that of one specialist area in relation to others; an analysis at the level of occupations goes nowhere deep enough. Ultimately, it is an issue of integrity – the integrity of *the product* itself and the derived integrity of those associated with its manufacture, whether they work in a factory or not. Take the example of Mercedes Benz in the 1950s. The received wisdom at that time was that there was no 'marketing' capital to be had in crash-testing programmes. The public, truth to tell, didn't want to know about safety; to be reminded at all that the motor car was anything less than a status symbol, or a virility-totem, or whatever. Mercedes went on crashing perfectly good cars into brick walls to see what happened to the engine; rolling them over to see where the roof collapsed and so on. They did it because, to the engineers in charge, it seemed the right thing to do if you wanted to build a better motor car. I don't suggest they neglected marketing, simply that at the heart of the enterprise was a devotion to the product itself which represented the glue that held the enterprise together spiritually as well as technically. The resultant car has integrity too – literally, it holds together under stress.

Now, motor cars are emotive things and it would be unfair to single out the British motor industry, without recognizing that many British firms nobly except themselves from the general rule that engineering and production have been too little in the minds of top management and finance, relatively speaking, too much. Wealth, like happiness, is often a by-product of some other enterprise. Let me contrast instead a British factory (although it could as easily been have an American one, though perhaps not French) devoted to making bread. This is an emotive product too. Bread seems to me to be a product about which people are likely to have feelings and opinions. Anyone who makes bread is bound to have a spouse who *buys* bread, so that the roles of producer and consumer may be readily understood in the context of each other.

At this particular factory, I was shown, with great pride, a remarkable, vastly expensive, largely automatic machine which makes 'slimmers' bread. When I enquired into the technology, it transpired that what the machine did was to get more *air* into the bread than the conventional breadmaking technology. Thinking of the complex technology, something prompted me to ask the relative cost to the customer of this new bread-and-air-mix loaf. Slimmers, it seems, may pay nearly twice as much for about half as must substance, in order to become less fat on the accustomed number of slices per day or, alternatively, stay just as fat on twice the slices. At the time I assumed that my informant, the 'manager', was demonstrating a form of wry, deadpan humour peculiar to the region in presenting the realities thus. Not so; he was all admiration for the cunning way in which technology and marketing together conspired to outfox the poor, dumb consumer. I declined to ask if his wife was slimming; I doubt the question would have gone home, even had I dared. He was, it seemed to me, a natural successor (scaled down) in the tradition of Drake.

I recount the tale for two reasons; firstly to illustrate the process of dissociation from the product, even a product with the social, political and Biblical associations of bread and, secondly, to highlight the truth that 'management', if it isn't entirely dissociated from end products, is bound to have different meanings in different settings. In the course of recent years I have been associated with work in industries with such diverse end products as military aircraft, computers, raw minerals, bank notes and money policy, food, advertisements, amongst many others, In each, the culture of the organization was different and to a more or less degree in harmony with the end product. Whatever the accepted definition of management, the activity of managing (i.e. Management I) is distinctive.

The same thing applies to that particular class of institutions whose primary throughput is people (schools, transportation systems, hospitals etc.). Here too there is an affinity between organizational culture and the kind of processing performed on the customers; here too, as in hospitals, the 'product' is often dealt with by an act of dissociation. In conventional industry, military aircraft, for example, are often thought of in terms of aesthetics – 'Isn't she beautiful?' – even though *her* purposes are not. Indeed, it is a trick of dissociation to assign *femininity* to a machine for destruction, as though it were an ocean liner. Cigarette manufacture is dealt with similarly, usually by 'diversification'. Scratch a manager in the tobacco industry and he will enthuse about the corporation's brewing, super-market, packaging, perfumery etc. interests. It is as if the *function* of diversification is to have interests *other* than cigarettes, for obvious reasons.

Now it doesn't follow, although it might, that being good at one thing will ensure success in another. There are some people with the talent for this sort of switching but they are rare and the talent is not limitless. It certainly doesn't follow that an entire organization can adapt to a new business – a new set of assumptions about the different sorts of end products and different means of producing them. The 'generalist' myth says that once you have risen above a certain point you can do it all, but that is to deny the necessity for having in your bones an instinctive understanding of all the processes of your trade. Indeed, the generalist approach says you *ought* to be above all that. Professor John Morris of the Manchester Business School tells the tale of the well-known chief executive who, on being asked, in front of a large luncheon group, a most simple question about his corporation's attitude to employees, passed the enquiry to his labour relations manager with the audible comment, 'No sense keeping a dog and barking yourself!' Note also the newspaper report about the senior cigarette executive appointed to run the ailing British Leyland: 'He has been in the tobacco industry most of his working life. He admitted yesterday at a press conference that he did not know "too much about the motor industry, but I do know how many beans make five in the business world!"'

The five beans There is an element of magic in the idea of the five beans, as though they might be some form of talisman, helpful in working miracles. Indeed, there is a persistent charmed circle of senior 'names' who tend to be plugged in, by the nation, as it were, to problem situations in problem British industries. Here, clearly, there is a 'call' in the 'national interest', involving people whose earning levels make a £30,000 salary drop of derisory importance. It isn't at all clear how people enter the circle. It certainly is not much connected with an entrepreneurial track record nor, perhaps more

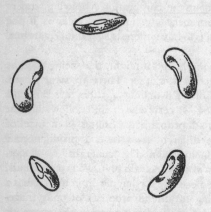

The five beans (arranged in a charmed circle)

important, any deep understanding of manufacturing processes and cultures. More likely, it is a function of whether or not you are known by those in the extreme centre, either those in the civil service and/or the main political parties. The trick is to become a 'name' in the first place (a subject covered more fully in Chapter 7). Once you have done it, you are quite respectable; no longer 'in business' but helping the Government *with* business; a neat switch, from huckster to medico in one effortless move.

The problem with the charmed circles at the top of British industry is that they tend to drain all the magic away from the levels beneath where most of what really matters happens. If the gods descended to the production line, if they understood, for example, the process of establishing production standards, presumably they would lose their magic. The reality is that, if most of the 'names' in the high places of British industry did so descend, their abysmal ignorance of the fundamental nature of production would be exposed. I except the exceptions. It is a matter of record that in other countries, those with an engineering background rise more frequently to the top, retaining the while the engineer's fascination with matter – with the properties of matter, with what happens when you bend, join, press or stamp, mix and so on. To quote one Swedish manufacturing manager, 'It doesn't stay like a hobby for the British managers' (in manufacturing).

Is it just my imagination, or is it also the case that the average British factory is less spick and span, less often painted, irrespective of its age, than its Continental counterparts? Does it have pride invested in it in the same way? Is it, in its way, the spiritual temple of the enterprise, or is that the polished panelled boardroom? My assumption is that a factory has a special character and personality when senior management understand its detailed workings in their bones, and their hands; the system as a whole has a sense of integration in a way that a split-off 'marketing' and finance-dominated senior management can never achieve. To attempt to plug in a stranger, no matter how charmed his career to date, who knows nothing of the special quality of a particular manufacturing enterprise, of the details, looks, to other cultures, like gimmickry or witchcraft.

I have argued in Chapter 3 that Britain may be thought of as, dominantly, a dependency culture. This idea is reinforced by the existence of the charmed circles and by the debilitating incapacity of the British to sack incompetents. If incompetence is abroad, the 'system' is always to blame and the incompetent himself is not to be sacked because no one *told* him what to do – so the error is always compounded by half a dozen others. This difficulty in locating anybody who is able or prepared to assume full responsibility for dealing with the client or consumer leads inevitably to the charmed top. Only the top man is really responsible and even here, when disasters occur, a special form of 'resignation', which is not really a resignation at all, has become the fashion. The belief that someone, somewhere (God knows who) will see it all to rights, despite the evidence, is a powerful manifestation of dependence. If we find ourselves depending on someone who knows little or nothing of manufacture, manufacturing sites, and manufacturing people, then we are better off depressed.

What is the comparative evidence? In Sweden, the only country for which comprehensive data of this kind exists, survey evidence shows that engineers form the effective backbone of industrial management. Graduate engineers constitute two-thirds of those graduates in top posts and even outnumber natural scientists by seven to one in the technical development area. A little under half of all chief production managers are graduate professional engineers and 86% are qualified as engineers of one sort or another. 30% of all job holders in all functions at this level are graduate professional engineers. Two-thirds of all graduate job holders in Level 2 jobs (just below the functional chief in a plant) are graduate *engineers*. Nearly a quarter of all graduates at this level are in production. In general, graduate engineers are known and accepted to have a high status in Swedish society generally, partly through the good reputation and position of the technical universities in Stockholm and Götenborg.

In Germany, too, more managers are university graduates than in Britain and more of them have studied subjects relevant to industrial management, especially law, business economics and engineering. The largest single group, in terms of university specialism, are the engineers. In comparison to Britain, the German engineering students, before entering university, have a school performance level which is at least average compared with students in other disciplines. That is, German management includes more engineers and they are more able, as judged by performance at school. In comparison with Britain, more German managers also hold post-graduate qualifications. Similar situations obtain in other European countries. In general, on the Continent, it is clearly all right to be associated with production and, by extension, with factories.

Is the situation likely to change in Britain? It is not difficult to log the applications for university places to ascertain fashions amongst students. The universities are on the whole powerless to resist these, often sudden, swings of fashion. At some universities now, despite many unfilled places in engineering, the demand for places in medicine and law far outstrips supply. Why do they all want to be doctors and lawyers – are we really so sick and litigious or does it just mean that these are known to be the most prestigious rip-offs in an already cynical society? Some argue that it is wrong to press for more investment in an ailing manufacturing sector when the true British genius is for money management and creative agency-type work, especially as Western Europe is already over-producing in relation to actual need. But the infuriating thing is that manufacturing *can* work in Britain and does sometimes, especially under alien management. Given strong and purposeful leadership together with a concern for standards, the British worker, as anyone else, responds superbly. Because middle and junior management seem not to have either authority, confidence or integrity, because their managers are hardly integrated with the production process, they do not supply leadership. Not surprisingly, for we all require leadership, the shop steward emerges from the shadows as the surrogate leader. If the foreman or first-line manager comes to represent *lack* of leadership, *absence* of effective control and *inadequate* engineering skill and experience, who better as surrogate leader than the shop steward, a man who seems at least to be clear about what he is doing and involved with it?

Let me illustrate my paean on production management with a moral tale – the saga of Platt Clothiers Ltd (as recounted by Peter Gorb in a recent issue of *Management Today*) – a firm unknown to most people unless they happen to purchase *overcoats* for Marks and Spencer, Burton, Hepworth, C & A, Dunns, Debenhams or (in the USA) Macy and Brooks Bros – that is, the *cognoscenti* of the clothing industry. I choose it because, whilst the British may easily become excited, to the point of hysteria, by high technology manufacturing ('science'), the overcoat is both more homely and, probably, useful. Monty Platt is chief executive and sole owner of one of the few successful companies in what is a fast declining business in a centrally-heated, automotive society. It is a small company but in the Government league table of clothiers, it bats near the top: in 1973 profits were £323,000 on sales of £2.5 million, or around 12% – a return on capital of about 30%. Since 1974, the firm has managed, in lean times, to double sales value and more than maintain volume. Recently, the firm sold £300,000 worth of overcoats to the USSR; selling anything to the Russians is a feat – but overcoats!

On the surface, there is nothing particularly interesting about Platt Clothiers Ltd except its success. The nineteenth-century building near Manchester contains people, machines and systems superficially as rough and ready as the building itself. But beneath the surface is an efficient and tightly controlled beehive of activity where everyone lives and thinks *overcoats* If you ask Monty Platt about his sales and marketing organization, he will reply, 'My overcoats sell my overcoats.' At 11 a.m. each morning a bell sounds, and anyone who wants to moves into the design office to have a look at yesterday's production. A random sample of overcoats is there to touch, try on, pull apart, mull over; and the boss is there talking overcoats to his dispatch manager, junior production staff and his designers. In fact, the business centres around the design room where new ranges are constantly being assessed against production constraints, customer requirements and fashion needs. Monty Platt has managed to instil his enthusiasm for overcoats into everyone who works for him. Of course, he has to talk about 'marketing', 'personnel', 'production' and other such rarefied ideas; but no one there can be in any doubt about their essential context – overcoats. In that context, Monty Platt has nothing to learn about managing role boundaries – not for him the personnel man's first-name chit-chat about family and football; his relationship with employees is about *work* and for them it is about working for an outfit that knows what it is doing, cares about *that,* and does it well. No one at Platts would trade that for the more familiar mix of back-slapping and product disinterest.

What is the moral? Not all firms have the luxury of a single-product orientation nor the cosiness of an integrated, compact organization. But all firms make *something* and they differ wildly in how much care goes into *that*. If only they so organized themselves that the kinds of people with a feel for manufacturing, for making things and making them well, ended up in key positions of authority, the chances are that the whole situation would *feel* different. Such people have *integrity*, in the precise sense of that word in a manufacturing system, and they generate a feeling of integrity, in the broader sense, all around them. If you have integrity built in, role relationships tend to fall into place, including the roles of 'worker' and 'manager'. A Swedish chief executive put it to me – 'Why don't the British educate people *not* born in flower-beds?'

I am arguing that British industry, despite what is often said, is full of first-rate people, but often they don't get promoted. The ones that do are the ones who *seem* right to those already in the driving seat and *that* is not necessarily relevant to the job to be done. I don't suggest that those who have spent a life-time in production do not need a lot of 'bringing on', including training, in order to fill other and bigger roles. But, the problem for the teaching institutions is to get the production managers out at all. Nonetheless, at the end of the day, production people do have something inside them which is irreplaceable by training and which needs expression in boardrooms.

It is the same ingredient which will be found in the thousands of trendy cottage industries now thriving in Britain; that is, skilled craftsmen and designers making jewellery, fabrics, pottery and other such artefacts. It is, to some extent, a middle-class phenomenon, preferable, if you have any talent, to other professional callings, though more demanding and less financially secure. What is a jeweller's profession? Is he part of *Kunst* (to use the German classification for fine arts) or of *Technik* (i.e. manufacture)? Clearly, he is both, but in Britain he is bound to assert the former and deny the latter; he will certainly resist the idea that, if he builds up a thriving production facility, he has himself a small factory. That is another kind of place where, presumably, his skills would not be required or valued. He is wrong to think they are not required but, sadly, too often right in thinking he would not be wanted. One of the best British design consultancies got short shrift from the British car industry but is now being used to the hilt by Volkswagen. It isn't a total loss, but has to be counted as a partial one because it suggests that, although British design abhors manufacture, and vice versa, both designers and production managers can work perfectly well, in their separate ways, for foreigners. Nevertheless, it is clear that craftsmanship, standards and service are not dead in Britain; they have simply gone trendy.

It seems to me sad and even shocking that this split between craftsmen and industry should be taken so totally for granted (in Britain). Elsewhere, in Scandinavia for example, no such radical separation exists: there are solitary craftsmen, massive industrial concerns, and any number of half-way houses in between. And as a result, their products often have a coherence that we can only envy: not flashy 'styling' superimposed on manufactured goods, but objects from the hands of engineers who have taste and respect for craftsmanship, and from craftsmen who have an understanding and respect for engineers. In any society worth working in, this must surely be so. (Liam Hudson.)

In big organizations, the very idea of 'job' has gone trendy as well. In fact, many people don't talk about their jobs any more at all, but about 'roles'. Role is a fearfully difficult word to define clearly, which is one of its virtues if your heart isn't really in outputs. The predominance of the word 'role' and the decline of 'job' supports the idea I have put forward elsewhere that work is defined by the Briton in terms of relationships rather than outputs, just as education is about learning to *be* someone rather than to *do* something.

I find it hard to know whether deficiencies of design are more crippling than those of manufacture. Those who argue for separation of the functions and the according of proper status to the former are undoubtedly right. I was told once of the British car firm whose Belgian factory, otherwise marvellously productive, was markedly less successful than its British counterpart in putting in the windscreens of a particular rogue model so they actually stayed in place. Of course the thing ought to have been designed properly in the first place, but the British genius for muddling through was impressive just the same. It is beginning to be accepted that many British production engineers abhor preventative maintenance because it is so much *duller* than fixing a comprehensively broken-down machine. Britain is a fun culture, and that is lovable, but with a short-term view (fly now, pay later). The long-term results of inadequate preventative maintenance are not fun at all. As Hudson says, design and manufacture are twins – separate, but bound inevitably together.

The counter to the earlier argument about too few manufacturers in high places and too many accountants is supposed to be the example of preliquidation Rolls Royce, notorious for an abundance of engineering skills and no grasp of finance at all. It is no counter at all, it is the exception which proves the rule. The fact that engineering salaries at Rolls Royce were always too low shows that the decision to work there was always part-irrational, having much to do with prestige and little to do with economic commonsense. Rolls Royce then was the repository of all manner of projections about engineering excellence. It may have been, because of the snob associations of the name, one of the few places in Britain where manufacturing was given due significance, but to the exclusion of all else. As in other prestige industries, the besetting manufacturing sin was to push too far too fast. Again, this is an example of splitting – the binary mode of thinking which pushes people and organizations to the extremes and destroys the possibility of integration in the middle ground.

Sex and production management

As I write of production and production management, my mind strays to thoughts of sex. British industry is thought of as masculine in composition and spirit – a split-off sub-culture within a culture of Dependence. The women are to be found, if at all, in the personnel department (helping to clean up human relations messes created by the men in the line functions), in administration (straightening out other people's sloppy attention to detail), and on the line (taking care of the drudgery). In other words, women in industry are employed in housewifely roles because that seems to provide everybody else with the best sense of fit. The roles are supportive ones, ancillary to the main thrust of the work as it is usually thought of.

But, under the skin, production is just like gestation. The factory doesn't go away like the salesmen and engineers on the road; it sprawls on its site awaiting new impregnations of raw materials, components and orders every day. Every impregnation sets in train a complex and ordered process of coming together of bits and pieces and people, of taking shape and finally of birth as a finished product. At that point, daddy takes over again and the infant artefact sets out on its long journey to the rubbish heap. It follows that the best production managers, like mothers, tend to have an almost feminine capacity to sense that something terrible is going to happen, just before it does. But there are no female production managers, or at least very few, although some female people-managers may be found a little down the line, particularly if the line contains women. I know one such, rejoicing in the title of 'Factory Fore-lady' who rules her 'girls' with a benevolent rod of iron. Here there are *standards* few men would dare ask for and here too is a place to come to with a pregnancy out of wedlock and other such troubles. This particular lady advises her factory girls to doff their factory uniforms before going down to the town, else 'everyone will think you are just factory girls.' It is a neat and subtle trick and it works too.

I am not suggesting a wholesale replacement of men by women in top manufacturing jobs. It wouldn't work; but a time will have to come when more of the top people (of whatever sex) think and feel about their operations in much the same way as a mother of her brood or a housewife of her household. That, after all, is one main strand (*menager*) of our modern concept 'management'. If all you have at the top is overgrown technical boys playing trains and seeing the social system as an annoying constraint on the technical, then you get what we have had in Britain for many years past. You get trouble, roughly translated as 'labour relations' and, in the end, you may finally get some women posted to that department. I am saying no more than that organizational systems require Dependence so long as they employ people. Sadly, many of the people who succeed in fighting their way to the top are, in the end, poor receptacles for Dependence, even frightened of it. They can't be blamed, because the career system usually requires them to win their spurs by grappling with tricky Fight situations all the way up. In the end, their natural orientation to the Fight/Flight Basic Assumption has been reinforced by success. For them, hard, manipulative management is 'good' management.

It isn't, as a matter of fact, a particularly difficult matter to take one of these Fighters, provided he has a few brains, and alert him to the Dependency dimension. The odds are he is a delightful husband and father and his household is a veritable stronghold of Dependence. His problem is that, true to the tenets of binary thinking, he has split his life into its hard (Fight/Flight) and soft (Dependence) bits. The tragedy is that most of the management consultants and educators have never even *heard* of Dependence (though they rely on it all the time) and confuse the manager with a mass of technical tomfoolery he could probably do well without. The good golf pro doesn't tell you to remember ten things at once; he has the knack of picking out the one factor that compounds all the others and he homes in on *that*.

If production be, in some repects, feminine, marketing could be seen as quintessentially masculine. Here, the system projects out into its environment; it goes hunting for sustenance. The primary hunter is the salesman and ironically enough, the best of them are creatures of intuition. It has been said before that salesmanship is a promiscuous activity. The salesman must, in each encounter, simulate a depth of trust and feeling that he cannot possibly feel inside himself. Refusal feels personal, although technically it was the product to blame; it feels personal because the salesman uses himself to sell; presents himself almost like a work of art in each new encounter. Any sales manager (as every Madam knows of her charges) knows that the 'bad patch' is signalled by extreme difficulty in extricating oneself from one's favourite customers and a concomitant reluctance to take on new ones. Again, there aren't many saleswomen, outside of cosmetics and the like, yet it is much nicer to be seduced than raped; if you happen to be sold by a woman, it isn't easy to know if anyone has triumphed at all and, if so, who.

The most obvious link between production management and sales is the importance in both of the presence of those qualities, mostly intuitive, that we tend to associate with women. A further important link is that they do represent the main parts of a manufacturing enterprise; you make things and you sell them and all those other hangers-on, the accountants, the lawyers, the personnel people, the planners, the PR types, simply attend to details at the periphery. But the really important link between production and sales is the stark truth, in Britain, that they stand at the bottom of the status league table. It isn't exactly respectable to be in industry in the first place, but if you are, you can be half-way respectable so long as you stay away from production and sales; that is, the fundamental activities that give industry its identity. It is as if tennis were a respectable game, provided you never hit the ball. But, to be a ball boy, on the periphery, is perfectly OK. How has British culture got its industry into such an unholy paradox?

Again, reference to sex, and sex stereotypes, helps. If British culture is dominated by dependent assumptions, if the gods of the British mother country are feminine (unlike those of the Germans and the Americans) then where are the male gods? The answer is, of course, in industry, but in so puffed up and distorted a form as to be almost a joke. To work in the traditional professions, the 'caring' professions, the civil service and so on is seen as worthwhile and of *national* importance. To work in industry is felt as serving *sectional* interests, despite the efforts of propagandists since the turn of the century to sell the idea of industry as a 'national service'. To be sure, industry is an alien sub-culture, dominated by assumptions which put competence and efficiency before unquestioned caring, where it is sometimes best to be cruel to be kind. In a sense, this is what industry has to *teach* the nation, because the inability of successive governments to grasp nettles, to defer gratification, has been at the heart of Britain's troubles. Government has done to the people exactly what the well-meaning but misguided social worker does to her clients when she, by denying realistic Fight draws them ever closer and more dependently into the welfare net.

Yet industry, at its best, mobilizes masculine and feminine skills and attitudes; the best firms deploy caring and intuitive people in the key jobs of production and sales, just as the best parts of the caring and professional sectors occasionally understand that the job comes first and the employees next, competent or otherwise. But, in most of the caring professions, you care first for your own and the only loser in the end is the client, the public at large. Try to sack an incompetent headmaster, social worker, judge, government official and see how far you get. Listen to the conclusions of inquiries into almost unbelievable administrative incompetencies of the carers' managers (visible, like the tip of an iceberg, only when a small child is battered to death) – no one is really to blame, no one will be sacked; the 'system' is at fault and there will be *more* meetings, *more* committees involving *more* well-intentioned but woollyminded folk to try to make sure it doesn't happen again and, *inter alia*, to spread the culpability wider and thinner than ever. It is a distasteful thing to assert in Britain, but it is probably true that any system which never sacks its incompetents is fundamentally and irrevocably corrupt. Industry, to some extent anyway, knows this, yet, traditionally, 'corruption' – *in a narrower sense* – is thought to reside in industry.

Now, I am not complaining that Britain is a dependency culture, that would be pointless; nor that assumptions associated with hardness and masculinity are split-off and projected into industry. Up to a point, it makes sense; but what can be observed in Britain is an almost total split of masculine and feminine assumptions – a schizoid gulf which perfectly reflects the British version of binary thinking at its most simpleminded. The fundamental division of humankind into men and women is projected on to industry vs the rest. At the head of one sub-group, the second Queen Elizabeth and all she symbolizes, at the head of the others, Sir Francis Drake and all his infamous successors; a system in which one side pretends that caring about people doesn't really matter much and the other that nothing much else matters at all. It is largely pointless for 'professionals' to argue whether 'management' or 'unions' are the culprits when those same professionals project most of their hang-ups about standards, rigour and redundancy into industry as a whole.

To return to my original theme, the good factory has intuitive and housewifely bosses but not at the expense of standards. The good organization, as the good human being, is tough and caring, soft and hard, cruel and kind. The split-way things are is bad for the country, but it is also bad for the people. Very few that I meet like to deny their compassionate feelings, on the one hand, nor their understanding of standards on the other. As they see it, 'the system' compels them so to do while they are at work and to complain about it only in the pub afterwards. Apparently, we have no way of joining up the bits of ourselves into balanced wholes. The split is displaced into work and non-work; the bastard manager is a softy with his kids; the weak and over-indulgent professional carer a stickler for standards anywhere else. One thing is clear and that is that industry cannot be whole until society at large takes back into itself what has been projected into industry.

The product as the fount of authority

In the binary mode of thinking, therefore, there is the notion of a 'good', idealized society, part of which must do bad things (making and selling) to ensure economic survival, just as the army is called upon to do dreadful things under physical threat. You can, however, graduate from one part to the other. This version of events throws up two principal character types – the All-Round Man, who best represents the reflective, intellectual, existential values of the mother culture, and

Industrial Man. Industrial Man is of two types: the winners are buccaneers (cf., Drake) and have at least a sporting chance of achieving associate All-Round Man status. The losers are sometimes called 'cannon-fodder for industry' as though they are sent 'over the top' to be consumed in the fray.

All this keeps alive an obsession with economics and material things. Schoolteachers are exhorted to direct their best charges into industry, not for its intrinsic attractions, but because otherwise the country might go broke. But the truth is that the official All-Round Man is an effete apology for a human being, all head and no guts. Any human being without an appreciation of *things*, of matter, of nature (beyond bird-life) has been sold short. That is the significance of *products*; production of some kind, rather than simply relationships, is the ultimate source of authority in the world of affairs. At base, it is a philosophical or educational argument, not an economic one.

Nothing could illustrate this theme better than a short paper by Michael Hope, the one-time chairman of Crittall-Hope, a major British metal window manufacturer. This is a poignant, and remarkably frank, account of what it is like to be 'taken over' by people with not the least interest in products. To add to the poignancy, the predator was none other than Slater-Walker and the paper was written just before the spectacular collapse of that notorious pack of financial cards:

At a time when most of the country's industrial production is financed by issues of shares on the Stock Exchange it is only logical that control of industry should increasingly fall into the hands of people with a Stock Exchange outlook. 'The product we are going to make is MONEY,' said Mr Slater at his first Crittall-Hope board meeting, and this undoubtedly reflects the wishes of most Stock Exchange investors, who are far more interested in their dividends (or their capital appreciation) than in the products of the companies which they collectively own. This is not the attitude I should hazard of the men who founded most of the country's greatest industrial undertakings. Many of these have been built up by men who were predominantly and even passionately interested in the products they were making (or the services they were providing). If ever control of the country's industry falls exclusively into the hands of men whose sole interest is in the return on their investments British industry will become a duller, feebler, less resilient growth than it has been in the past.

As a postscript, when Slater-Walker finally off-loaded Crittall-Hope to yet another conglomerate the new owners announced that the window business was running at a loss. This was something that had *never* happened to the old management since the great slump of the 1930s.

The following diagram is a schematic representation of the difference between power networks and authority structures, a theme to which I shall return. If you feel powerless, and many people do, it is quite natural to become obsessed by power and to regard it as a scarce commodity which is being hoarded by somebody else – 'management' for example. Power relationships may be exciting but they are always potentially claustrophobic (the diagram illustrates, for example, the difference between shacking up with someone for as long as it suits you versus jointly entering into the institution of marriage). The *third corner* is the institutional framework and, when it works properly, it can relieve personal

1. A POWER NETWORK

2. AN AUTHORITY STRUCTURE

relationships of that claustrophobic quality (the good marriage is not fight-free, it simply has *high quality* fights). When the third corner is an object or a task (institutionalized in some form) all the better; it is no longer a matter of *masters* and *men* or winners and losers, but different *kinds* of *servants* to an over-arching task. But it can't work that way unless the object is dominant – unless the people really care about it and care about getting it right.

The good enterprise

It is time now to say something about those enterprises (not excluding schools, families, government departments, profes-sional practices, etc.) which actually succeed. Failure is fascinating; but success is instructive. All the best enterprises I have seen combine two qualities (I think they are necessary, not sufficient):

1 The top management, especially the top man, has the task in his/their guts – to the point of obsession. They are less concerned with 'managing' a system than with *doing* something in relation to an environment — having a *product* or output. They are generalists and specialists at the same time. (I remember working as a fairly lowly employee of the IBM Corporation in Australia. At that time I deplored the way the Management Review Committee in the USA – the holy of holies – concerned itself with detail out in the boondocks. Surely, I thought, they ought to stick to strategic matters. I see it better now – they were keeping their feet in the mud, or the fertilizer, and it made them better strategists.)

2 There is a *constitutional* sense in the organization. That is to say, someone has taken the trouble to institutionalize the arrangements under which people work – decision-making, grievance channels, lines of authority. Such attention to detail doesn't drive out conflict, but it ensures that most of the fights that do occur are *about* something of significance. Ask not if you *have* fights – do you have *efficient* fights? Of course, in an authority structure, you can change hats in mid-fight (at 5.30 pm) and go and have a beer together.

I exclude the quality of intelligence, because it is *assumed*; 1 and 2 (above) are intelligent *enough*.

The good enterprise (and the good boss) is therefore tough but fair. The good boss feels *entitled* to be tough, to insist on high standards, because he has his eye on the ball (the task, the product). He does not spare *himself* in the pursuit of quality and he tends *not* to see relationships at work as personal ones and therefore as 'tough' in an offensive way. The good boss is fair, not by personal dispensation, but because he has had the good sense to institutionalize the rules. They, however imperfect, are impartial – the same for everyone – and above all, written down – visible.

I often ask people how many bosses they have had (stock answer: five to fifteen) and then how many of them were really any good. Par for the course (if you are lucky) seems to be one or two. If you then ask what was it about them, you get a variety of answers, all reducible to 'tough but fair'. The good boss is indefinable, but people seem to know it when they see it. It is, of course, the same quality one finds in good parents, good teachers and in fact any figure of authority in any setting. Almost everyone seems to know this.

6 Management development – a new priesthood

As the foregoing chapters indicate, we have not quite got the hang of running big organizations yet. I doubt we have properly grasped the dynamics of any organization bigger than a village (beyond which human scale disappears). We certainly haven't worked out (except in wartime, which is why many people pine for those days) how to identify large numbers of people with a common purpose. It is easy enough to get large numbers of people *loyal* to an institution upon which they depend for survival, but that is not a matter of purpose. If there is a 'third corner' in such a dependent relationship, it is the idea of a club, and clubs simply exist to exist; they do not produce. (As I suggested in Chapter 5, many people at work are quite dissociated from the output of their employing organization and as consumption becomes more conspicuous and less defensible, that process is likely to accelerate.)

Further, we have signally failed, as a species, to throw up appropriate leaders reliably. It comes as a pleasant surprise when, every so often, a 'good man' – inspiring, dedicated and, above all, honest – rises to the top. Of course, it is not easy to define 'good' in this context, but most people seem to know it when they see it.

Modern industrial man is faced therefore by at least three pressing problems:

1 How to succeed, to get ahead/on top of the pile.
2 How to *follow*, to live with one's talents and to accept the authority of one's organizational superiors.
3 How to be creative; or to share in creative purposeful work.

Problems 1 and 2 have spawned 'management development' –

the principal means by which middle-aged executives are shepherded through their mid-life crises and the philosophical and emotional turmoils that go with them. Whether 'management development' has had anything to do with 3 is an open question.

The first reference I have been able to find to 'management development' in the UK occurs in 1951, typically in a document (the report of the Anglo-USA Productivity Study Team) recommending the import of American business practices to the UK. Management development, *as a process*, is not new of course. Managers have always lived, developed, rotated in, and passed away out of their organizational system. But new, since the war, is a body of specialists in this process, specialists usually to be found somewhere in the personnel department, though often near its periphery. When management development takes root, a common pattern is something like the diagram on p. 123.

But how can the suggestion that management development represents a new priesthood be supported? Religions perform many functions, but they all offer that hope, to the faithful, of a better life than the present sometime hereafter. Belief in this is central, often a necessary condition to bear the sacrifices of the meantime. In management development, as in religion, one finds that characteristic combination of public observance and private doubt – you may not be convinced, but you had better play it safe. 'Managers adopt the management development schemes as an obedient child might; in public, unquestioningly and with trust, but guardedly and with limited conviction in private.' Management development offers the middle-aged manager not only *a better life*, hence 'development' but life itself; 'an ordered work biography with a beginning, a middle and an end, with no disruption to its flow; a sort of "this could be your life".'

The phrase 'management development' combines two words of great pungency. 'Management' we have discussed before; in this case – the essence of management (Management I, II and III) – the realms *above* to which mortals aspire and, occasionally, ascend. 'Development' is something children do

Organizational growth

Concern about succession in high places

Creation of succession-based "management development" function

New M/D functionaries discover they have to deal with *all* the managers, not just the chosen few

Persistent demands for reassurance and legitimation from the middle aged un-elect

M/D pressed into motherhood activity—"development courses" "counselling" etc. etc.

University system wakes up to the possibility of empire-building in "management" studies, thus introducing respectability to the scene

M/D functionaries, unable to identify their clients, begin to come apart at the seams or to seek escape routes and it is a good thing too. It is the process by which we arrive at fantasized adulthood, as though one ever arrived finally anywhere. The infant who thought the world would be his at eleven transfers that assumption to leaving school or making management or whatever it might be. Always, there is another peak to scale but management development at least supplies a map. 'Management' and 'development' together are irresistible, linking, as they do, adulthood and childhood, heaven and earth, future and present. There is no corresponding specialism in management plateaux, management peaking or topping-out – the eyes are cast heavenwards always.

The men, hardly ever women, who preside over the rituals of management development are *good* men on the whole; men who bear a conscience on behalf of their fellows, who worry away at issues of equity, duty and trust. They do, after all, have to absorb the shocks of collision between the unforgiving world of work, competition and power politics, on the one hand, and, on the other, the internal world of individual hopes, aspirations and fears. The corporation, usually, can be expected to live for ever but, at some point, the individual is bound to recognize that, for him, time is going to run out. He has his own internal clock which won't necessarily keep time with the slow tick of the big corporate clock; this is not simply an important matter for the individual, it is *the* central issue for the corporate whole – how do you reconcile the corporate task system (decided on by no one in particular but by complex collective processes) with the needs and aspirations of the people who fuel its energies. More narrowly, how do you relate the corporate career system to the *life* systems of hundreds or thousands of employees and how, if at all, do you help them to understand that relationship?

These are proper worries for the chief executive, if he has the sense and stomach for it; otherwise it may be, inappropriately, delegated to somebody else, usually in 'personnel', perhaps in management development. If that person combines a caring proclivity (he is bound to be chosen for just that) with inadequate authority to carry through so central a task then it will

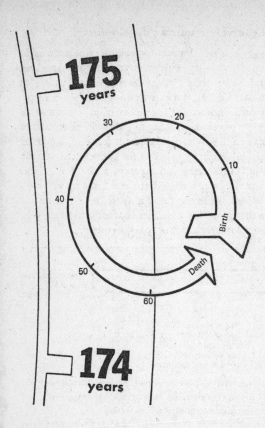

be no surprise to find, to quote one social scientist, 'Management development people having coronaries on behalf of their
organizations'. I well remember, at the tender age of twenty-
six, being offered my first post in management development. I
had not the faintest idea what the phrase meant yet found it
reassuringly familiar-sounding, almost soothing, like a mantra.
It took many years to grasp that it was more a faith than an
activity. At the time, I must have struck someone as a nice
chap; too nice by half, I assume now.

Human stock control vs human development

What the management development specialists are *supposed* to do may vary, but the job description invariably incorporates two fundamental ideas; one, ensuring the timely *supply* of replacement management stock wherever and whenever vacancies occur (what one eminent teacher calls 'human stock control') and, two, maximizing the *developmental* potential of each of the people in the system. The one is for 'management' (for the corporation) and the other is for 'development' (for the people) and it is unheard of, in my experience, for the job description to contain even a hint that these aims may, sometimes, conflict. Management development is a solidarity concept because the possibility of such a conflict is so studiously ignored, in practice and, for the most part, in theory.

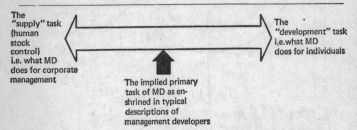

The "supply" task (human stock control) i.e. what MD does for corporate management

The "development" task i.e.what MD does for individuals

The implied primary task of MD as enshrined in typical descriptions of management developers

Practitioners, by the way they choose to operate, position themselves somewhere on a continuum between the 'supply' and 'development' poles, according to the prevailing organizational culture.

Where did management development, the specialism, not the process, come from? Where else but from the USA, the fount of British management ideology since World War II? In a survey made by the American Industrial Conference Board in 1946 it was revealed that the percentage of industrial companies operating in the United States which had management development programmes was so insignificant it was not worth recording. A similar survey just seven years later disclosed that 30% of the companies canvassed operated such programmes and the figure was to rise to 54% in 1955. What did the phrase mean in the USA in those early days, and was it anything like its British inheritance ten to fifteen years later? All the evidence suggests that the Americans had their eyes on economics, growth and competence in the depleted post-war years and that the management development movement was about fuelling an economic growth that was felt to be inevitable and preparing for the fight for world trade for which the Americans were spoiling. The Americans, in other words, needed more managers and this deadpan assessment (from Riegal in 1952) probably sums up the American approach accurately: 'For the period immediately ahead the companies whose experience this report reflects see *executive* development as one way to improve current operations and net earnings. For the longer term the companies see executive development as a contribution to their survival under competitive conditions.'

In fact, management development started life as 'executive development'. The main American writers (Bower 1949, Mace 1950, Riegal 1952, Hooher 1952 and Planty and Freeston 1954) all refer almost exclusively to executive development, which can be safely assumed to direct attention to the top end of the organizational hierarchy. Note the attempt to get the words straight in Planty and Freeston, writing in 1954:

Q What is the distinction between Industrial Training and Development?

A In recent years use of the word 'training' has more and more been restricted to activities of *wage earners* and *operatives* and 'development' has been increasingly applied to the training of *professional people*, *supervisors* and *executives*. The distinction is based upon levels served. Now and then one meets different attempts to distinguish between training and development, here the difference is one of method. Training is considered to be formal classroom group activities and development is thought of as an individual on-the-job approach.

Q What is Executive Development?

A Executive development is the planned improvement of high-level management in those understandings, attitudes and activities that enter into or influence their work relations.

It was left to a European (Drucker, an Austrian) to set out the creed in its more familiar, legitimatory, form.

Management development is also necessary to discharge the elementary *responsibilities the business enterprise owes to society* . . . increasingly it is to business that our citizen looks for the fulfilment of the *basic beliefs and promises of society*, especially the promise of *equal opportunity*. Manager development from this point of view is little but a technical name for the means through which we carry out a *central* and *basic part of our social beliefs and political heritage* . . . management development is another way by which management *discharges its obligations* to make work and industry more than a way of making a living. By offering a challenge, and opportunities for the individual development of each manager to his fullest ability, the enterprise discharges, in part, the *obligation to make a job in industry a way of life* (Drucker, 1954.)

An executive of Standard Oil of New Jersey, writing in 1949, put it more succinctly:

Some companies have adopted the title 'management development' (rather than executive development) which, in many respects, I like better. Management implies organization as well as personal leadership. Besides, there are usually more managers than executives; therefore the target is larger and *more easily recognized by the men down the line*.

If we combine the statements of Drucker and the gentleman from Standard Oil the argument can be put thus: management development is potentially very moral indeed (Drucker; external guru) and it is likely to impress subordinates (GSO; in-company personnel specialist). In this form, it would prove irresistible to British industry and it was fairly soon afterwards that its serious migration across the Atlantic began. The uses to which it was then put depended on the realistic situation in Britain – continued economic and industrial decline combined with a dogged determination to behave as if growth was still the name of the game.

Of course, by the late fifties, British management thought was already in the throes of Burnham. If it was white heat you wanted, then management development and management education seemed to make sense. Insofar as management development was the in-company manifestation of the belief in renewed industrial growth it ought logically to have been about efficiency, competence and economic performance. But, from all the evidence, British managers were not really in an aggressive mood – home sales were still holding up, living standards, including those of managers, were still rising and the political leadership was in no mood to rock the boat – 'You've never had it so good!' In fat times, there were now relatively *more* managers in *larger* organizations, expecting to be looked after *more*. Management development, at this point, was part of the maintenance package; one way of reassuring the managers and holding them close to the organizational bosom. Notably, in-company management development, as with 'personnel', has thrived only during periods of economic expansion. For personnel, this has also meant, historically, periods of labour shortage.

Management development is then the most irresistible of motherhood concepts. It ought also to be seen as the logical outcome of the British management movement. How are the practitioners in this new and arcane specialism to behave? What might be relevant modes of operation and what might they be based on? Recent research tends to indicate that practitioners revert, in their conscious and unconscious minds, to a number of very familiar models indeed. In a major study of the management development arrangements of ten big British firms, it transpired that management developers described themselves and their work in terms of three predominant analogues – the military, the family and the school.

The military model The archetypal military-style management development operation is one where paper is all; where, provided the appraisal system and the succession charts are kept flowing like a vast alimentary system, all is assumed to be well. Here it will be hardly necessary ever to *talk* to a manager, but the walls will be festooned with gaily-coloured campaign-like charts capable of locating everybody, including rank and number, at a glance. This is a world of known and static jobs, rather than developing and fluid roles. If the manager doesn't fit he must somehow be engineered so that he does, or a replacement part found elsewhere. The paperwork will locate the perfect man all coded and maybe even computerized. Clearly, the military model is located at the 'supply' end of the spectrum;

development in this setting really means job training to fit known and familiar slots. Not surprisingly, the military model is associated with certain kinds of organizations and certain kinds of people, namely big, stable, and bureaucratic organizations and those people who went straight from World War II into personnel work on the shared assumption that the army knows a thing or two about handling men. Whether there are new cohorts of military-style replacement personnel folk coming along, without benefit of carnage, only time will tell.

The family model The second analogue is an extended family one. Here much of the effort of the management developer is devoted, again not necessarily consciously, to sustaining in everybody's mind the vision of the small, self-contained and intimate unit that the organization may once have been. Here the underlying assumptions are of sibling rivalry and succession through the blood. Not surprisingly, family companies and those recently so, tend to hold these assumptions, but, even in very big firms, the idea of a blood-line may be extended to those who look right and know how to behave; perhaps an adoption model. Here one may find a management developer in a vast organization reassuring managers he has never seen before and may never see again that 'before you came in here you may have been just a name but now (holds up plastic-covered personnel form with attached mugshot) we know you.' Incredibly, it appears to work.

The school model The last analogy is the school one, and bearing in mind the British trust in 'education' as the healing balm for all manner of ailments, a powerful one. It appears to take two principal forms, firstly the 'civilizing' approach and secondly the 'updating'. In either case the emphasis is, relative to the military and family models, on the classroom rather than in the paperwork and trappings of management development. The civilizing approach is a direct reflection of the British educational system and aims to knock the rough edges off uncultured chaps who are destined for high places – 'round-shouldering them' to quote one cynic in the trade. Otherwise it teaches the young how to behave in high places – 'It was like going into the upper school' – with reference to a middle management course. Here, of course, the external university-based management courses are pressed into service, the more Oxbridge-like, the better. The 'updating' approach is a speciality of American firms. The assumption here is that, no matter how broken down by age and other forces, no matter how empty of ambition, the manager must be treated as if he were, dewy-eyed and bushy-tailed, setting forth on the management journey for the first time. There is a close correlation between this assumption and corporate growth; if the corporate growth goes up and up, so must the managers too. In such firms, the annual updating course has become a need, a hypodermic syringe direct into the psyche.

There is an additional phenomenon, difficult to locate according to the main analogies and that is a kind of ceremonial activity associated with the training of 'new managers'. This kind of rite may be peculiar to Britain and perhaps the USA because the entry into the portals of 'management' is made so portentiously in those cultures. The non-manager, or proto-manager, has to be made over into the image of management, whatever it is. In the military, it would be represented by the rise from NCO status to the officers' mess; in the family, an initiation, perhaps the coming of age or the Bar Mitzvah; in education, the 'new managers course' or such like. The individual doesn't simply move from one kind of job to another, he *passes over*.

The point about all these models is that they are rooted in society and its values. They provide a way, in the subconscious and partly-conscious mind, of giving a sense of familiarity and order to an imponderable task (i.e. 'management development') wrapped up in an almost meaningless phrase. We should reflect that the big organization is a quite modern phenomenon, at least since people started going to work with some expectation of a 'career' in the modern sense. In a country like Britain where bigness is culturally despised in the first place and the purposes of the enterprise felt to be without legitimacy, then it is no surprise that the 'career' may supplant the primacy of work itself.

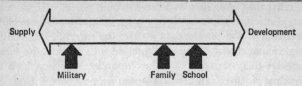

All the models of management development are associated with both 'supply' and 'development' activity, but the *essence* of each may be pinpointed nevertheless. In all except the Military model, the management development practitioner prefers to regard himself as being primarily in the personal development business.

On the Continent, it could be argued that one of the principal constraints on production is people's determination to look after their own best career interests; in Britain, that the necessity to produce is a burdensome constraint on getting ahead. This is reflected in the comments of Swedish general managers about their British managers – 'It is hard to get them to talk about work at all but they always say their ambition is to be managing director – our Swedish managers are more modest!' In fact, when British managers talk like this, I tend not to believe them. More than likely, they are saying what the fantasy-American manager is assumed to say.

If the primary task of the British firm is to elevate certain of its members to new statuses in society, then it is hardly surprising that 'management development' takes on a special meaning in Britain, vis-à-vis other countries. Nor is it surprising that management developers become a priesthood, regulating, as they purport to, traffic between the nether regions and the hoped-for realms above. In many ways it is as if, despite the obvious ironies, industry recreates a class structure within itself, including an aristocracy. I have a heart-rending recollection of a meeting of personnel managers of a big British firm being addressed by their managing director about promotion policy. His argument was that since the 'raft of graduates' started flooding in from the universities, it had become well-nigh impossible for outstanding men (like, for example, a number of the current directors) to work their way up to the top carrying with them a deep-rooted grasp of the business, especially in manufacture. One personnel manager, warming to the managing director's theme, agreed the firm had to 'fulfil its social responsibilities', as though promoting the odd non-graduate from within was an act of mercy, chargeable out of the charities budget. I fear the managing director never quite got his point across. It turned out he wasn't a graduate, of course, though much wiser than his bemused and presumably graduate colleagues.

7 The informal world of management development

The patron and protégé

All the main models of management development impose a logic and legitimacy upon what happens in reality. The military model imposes the logic of seniority, the family model legitimacy of the blood-line and the school the justification of knowledge. It is important for everyone to believe, whether they succeed or not, that success is linked with some kind of logic and beholden to some notion of legitimacy. To put it another way, it is psychologically intolerable, having risen, without a trace, to the heights, to be badgered by doubt that you do not really deserve it and it is equally insupportable for the failure to continue to believe that there, but for the grace of a little chicanery, he might have gone. American research suggests that there is a positive correlation between the enthusiasm with which senior executives espouse the *formal* management development system and the vigour with which they operate the informal patronage network on the side. Of the three management development models, the family one comes nearest to reflecting this mixture of formal primogeniture and informal favouritism. What's more, the formal and informal appear to be capable of coexisting fairly successfully, provided the judgement of the senior executives is sound. Sensible patronage works a lot faster than the best bureaucratic vetting and promotional procedures.

Apart from anything else, patronage satisfies very deep-seated needs in both patron and protégé. In my more jokey moments, I have recommended to the hopeful the seeking out of useful senior men who, by chance, have sired nothing but daughters, the more the better. Any young man, visiting such a household, knows the almost conspiratorial way in which any passably interesting male is ingratiated by the surrounded parent. I don't think this is a sexist observation; it is, alternatively, only natural when surrounded by men to pine for a woman.

Having dealt with the peculiarities of formal systems, it is necessary to say something about the informal. The problem is how. Some years back I aspired to being amusing about it all after the fashion of *How to Succeed in Business Without Really Trying* and numerous subsequent imitators. The problem for the comedians and the would-be comedians is that the joke is tasteless. True comedy is rooted in pathos and tragedy and it is no joke what is happening to legions of middle level executives in all kinds of large bureaucratic organizations. Whatever they are supposed to be doing by way of *work* – i.e. outputs – they contrive to behave as if they were still a junior in the army, an adolescent at home or a spotty student in school. The management development institutions and procedures usually serve only to reinforce this sense of familiar, dependent surroundings.

The anatomy of success

I used to do a talk for middle managers based on the anthropology of management systems, drawing on every known study of the components of career success. Oddly, it was, and remains, an understudied subject, possibly because it is too simple and too interesting to attract the average social scientist. There is, of course, the problem of defining success. The trickiest aspect of this is the reality that people define success in quite different ways at different points of their lives. Neither do they seem to be very good at predicting what their version of success will be ten years hence, otherwise their behaviour in the meantime might be more rational and less destructive.

The track record question and the mid-life crisis I see these definitions as ringed around the 'track record question'; a question which most people ask themselves, consciously or subconsciously, in mid-life. It runs something like this. 'I know all the things I *can* and *might* do and all the things I promised myself I *would* do but now, taking into account what I *have* done, is it really very likely that I *will* do them all?' For most of us, the answer to this is a flat 'no' and the result of asking the question out loud is depression. Whatever fantasies were kept alive, the individual now has to recognize that he *is* what he has become; his very substance is the fruit of his life's history; you are, in fact, what you did. I don't refer to depression here as a sickness; on the contrary, a man would have to be crazy not to become depressed by such truths. What he then does with this depression, otherwise known as the mid-life crisis, is a matter of redefining 'success' for that latter half of his life.

One of the unkinder charges which may be laid at the door of the post-war exponents of management education and management development is that they have unwittingly gone into collusion with middle managers to behave as if the mid-life crisis and by extension, death, didn't exist. Far from helping managers to come to terms with their realistic states, psychological and situational, they have engaged them in all manner of hopeful busynesses to ensure they never think about it at all. Of course, management educators and management developers have their own problems about mid-life and one way to ward off one's own latent depression is to deny its existence in one's clients. At any rate, eminent thinkers such as Jaques argue that if the realistic depression of mid-life is not faced up to and worked through successfully, the ultimate cost is likely to be a latter half of life characterized by depressive chaos, confusion, feelings of persecution and rage and progressive personality deterioration. Such deterioration is likely to be accompanied by manic defences of hyper-activity, intellectual dishonesty, heightened arrogance, ruthlessness concealing envy and fantasies of omnipotence. There can be few subordinates who have not encountered some or all of these in superior managers past.

Capacity vs opportunity As Jaques and Erikson have pointed out, these problems are associated with the approach of death; the moment when death ceases to be merely an idea and takes on a tangible reality. At that point, time becomes a precious commodity – a commodity consumed by use. Tomorrow becomes a non-negotiable currency; if you don't use it tomorrow, it is gone for ever. Of course, the mid-life crisis happens to coincide with the period of life when executives in organizations are either experiencing accelerated promotion or dealing with *not* experiencing it. Ideally, two things occur simultaneously:

1 *The individual's value system moves from shallow, other-directed motivations to more deep-seated inner-directed ones, seeking to express his talents in the achievement of important* ends (important to others as well; now he is aware of some kind of constituency beyond immediate subordinates). Now, he moves towards what Erikson calls 'generativity' – a phase of wishing to leave behind him something of value, to make a creative contribution to his world.

2 He moves, by promotion, nearer the centre of the organization where opportunities to do creative and important things multiply. This is the moment when a man or woman moves beyond the technical requirements of work and senses the many overlapping constituencies of the modern organization. Almost anyone can be an adequate management *technician*, fewer can become good leaders, and fewer still can *also* grasp and handle the role of *trustee* on behalf of those many constituencies. For one thing, to do so it is necessary to grasp that things really can be changed and in ways never dreamt of before. This is commonly referred to as *vision*.

The problem for the management population and hence for management development, is that this conjunction of readiness and opportunity is rare. Not everyone moves, in mid-life, into 'generativity' in the way described. A great many people simply carry on as before, perhaps more frenetically and less gracefully. For such people, there is no qualitative change in mid-life; no enlargement of the meaning of it all, but rather an acceleration of effort in old pursuits – getting ahead, familiar forms of competition with familiar adversaries and so on.

Let me introduce now yet another continuum – the Work

Survival Continuum (linked here specifically with the mid-life crisis):

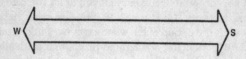

| W | S |

The work mode i.e. the capacity and desire to 'work through' mid-life to some new, inner directed perception of life's purpose, outside oneself. The adversary is death itself; it cannot be defeated but it may be coped with through absorption in valued work.

The survival mode i.e. the mobilisation of psychic defences against the 'work through' together with the displacement of energy into other-directed, competitive, familiar activity. The adversaries are career competitors and those who threaten conventional 'success'.

Naturally, survival-types are capable of work and 'workers' may have to cope with, to a greater or lesser extent, survival-type activity, but, on balance, people may be seen to skew in one direction or the other during their thirties. In mid-life, the individual is unusually at risk of being drawn into survival-behaviour in avoidance of the *work* of coming to terms with the passage of time. Some people do not, in fact, survive this period. Jaques points out that 'the closer one keeps to genius' amongst artists of undoubted greatness, the more one finds a high statistical incidence of premature death in the late thirties (Mozart, Raphael, Chopin, Rimbaud, Purcell, Baudelaire, Watteau) followed by low incidence between forty and forty-five.

'Workers' are good people to work for because a relationship with them may rise above the simply personal. The Work-boss may have already discovered, or be in the process of discovering, some vision of a better world outside himself, towards which one may join in striving. Conversely, the Survivor-boss offers an intense personal relationship, possibly exciting but always vulnerable because, after it is severed, there is nothing left (see fig. p. 138).

Whatever the potential stuff of Workers and Survivors, the number of niches in the highest reaches of organizations is

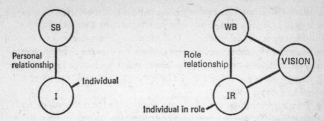

limited. When an organization starts, its task (i.e. work) will be foremost in the minds of its members because it has been set up to *do* something. If it grows, it will come increasingly to be seen by outsiders as a place where one may *get a job*, rather than a place where one may join in the prosecution of a particular task. *Getting a job, per se*, is a Survival activity. When the organization becomes bigger, opportunities to share in the *direction* of work on the task diminish relative to the whole. Taking the twin axes of Work/Survival and opportunity/no-opportunity, there are four main possibilities: see table on page 141.

If some are bound to fail, then how do people cope with the realization that they are not to be, if ever they aspired to, one of the elect? An indication is provided by the famous study (reported in *Science* in 1968) of all 270,000 male employees of the Bell System Co in America. The study linked, simply, job achievement, educational background (as an indicator of aspiration) and incidence of coronary heart disease (as an indicator of stress). The expectation, and the folklore, was that it is the hard-driving successes at the top that crack up. Over this huge population, coronary rates per thousand per annum were:

Top Executives:	1.85	Foremen:	4.52
General Area Managers:	2.85	Workers:	4.33
Supervisors/Local Area Managers:	3.91		

More significant still, the non-college educated men who had risen to the top were virtually immune and the college men who rose no higher than foreman died off, relatively speaking, like flies.

These musings leave us with three important ideas:

1 What kills you off, or screws you up, is falling seriously short of your *own* estimate of who you are or who you might have been or what you might have done with your life. That estimate, partly in the subconscious for most, goes (except perhaps for the true jungle fighters) way beyond questions of material sucess, and it tends to gell in mid-life.

2 Chance plays an enormous part in career progression. It probably shouldn't, but it does.

3 Very large numbers of dangerous people ascend to the top of many institutions. (Dangerous because not properly *institutionalized*; so consumed by ambition and survival needs that their dedication to common purposes cannot be relied upon.)

I noted much earlier on that the big bureaucracy and the linked idea of an orderly 'career' are historically quite new. Management development has a lot to answer for if it contrives to divert people's attention, especially the Bs, Cs and Ds (see table), from *work* and into such Survival considerations. As the economies of the developed nations start to peak out, people, if they are lucky enough to find employment at all, are going on have to find their 'motivation' in work itself.

Earlier I argued that British society assumes industry to be sectional, selfish and corrupt. There is too much truth in that for comfort, but not so much as to justify massive projections of those aspects into industry. At least, we may argue, management development should have an *opinion* on who the appropriate leaders of industry should be. In a culture of mutual distrust and envy, we clearly need more people in high places psychologically capable of *giving* and of constructing something bigger and more lasting than their own material success. In fact, this is saying no more than that we ought to promote reasonably well-adjusted people if we want reasonably sane, well-adjusted organizations. It looks like a simple matter but it isn't because so many nice people can be found who sincerely believe that a half-demented, power-crazed dynamo, persecuted by his past is what good management is all about. It is the Drake effect again, reinforced by a fantasy about the American miracle, cropping up in the oddest places. I have *seen* people select managers they didn't like and didn't trust because they were Drake-like, because they represented in fantasy the medicine that tastes bad and so must be good for you.

Career more successful than average	Career less successful than hoped/expected
'Workers'	'Workers'
A. This is, of course, the ideal case. The individual has the will, the talent, the philosophical base and, in mid-career, the *chance* to strike a blow, to build and leave behind him something of value which extends beyond his own material success.	B. Here, people with the psychological capacity for leadership roles do *not*, by chance or because the Survivors fight too well or cunningly, achieve them. Energy is redirected (perhaps too late) to other forms of work or consumed in dealing with depressive frustration. The individual wants to, and could, strike a blow for worthwhile causes, but has no effective vantage point from which to do so.
'Survivors'	'Survivors'
C. These are the power-system people of the 'rat pack', hard-driving, successful and amoral. Riven by internal insecurity they are increasingly subject to envy of others more internally secure than themselves and unwilling to promote any but their own kind. Most of the well-known *entrepreneurs* are like this.	D. These are failures; failing either to achieve a position of stature in life, failing to find a vocational niche appropriate to talent and aspiration, and failing to cope with feelings of rage and envy about it all. Here frustration tends to be projected outwards on to any convenient scapegoat or 'bad object', sometimes 'management'.

The wares of management development differ, and ought to differ, according to these four populations. The people in A for example require no more than an occasional hand in viewing their systems from different and perhaps more helpful perspectives. The Cs are suckers for 'motivational' packages, otherwise, ways of getting subordinates to do whatever will most reinforce their empires. The As and Cs may be assumed to be managers or fulfilled specialists and the Bs and Ds probably simply workers, or junior managers whose careers have come to a plateau prematurely.

The luck of the Irish One of my favourite studies, conducted by Egan and Barron in Ireland, got round the problem of defining success most elegantly. Egan knew that, in so tight a society as Dublin, there were very few people of major account and everyone tended to know who they were. The researchers' response was to ask everyone who were the prime-movers of Irish industry and, sure enough, they came up with the predicted forty or so people. It wasn't a very 'scientific' approach but there can be no doubt it was effective in sifting out the people who mattered. Having done so, they proceeded to ask the forty if they might have a thorough look at them in order to figure out why they had done so well. Was it birth, education and breeding, psychological make-up, or just luck? Characteristically, they all said (in effect), 'Yes, please, I have often wondered myself.'

The career speedometer The details aren't particularly important. The general importance of the study is that it dealt with the elusive issue of *luck*, the chance conjunction of man in a state of readiness and situation which sets off an almost irreversible chain-reaction – a kind of forced upward draft which only the most incompetent or unambitious are likely to resist. One

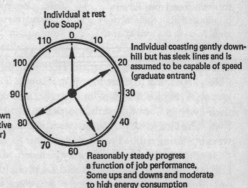

The career speedometer

Individual at rest (Joe Soap)

Individual coasting gently downhill but has sleek lines and is assumed to be capable of speed (graduate entrant)

Individual out of control down 1 : 4 gradient speed cumulative no engine braking (high flyer) (i.e. job results irrelevant)

Reasonably steady progress a function of job performance. Some ups and downs and moderate to high energy consumption (typical manager)

social scientist coined the idea of the accelerated 'career speedo-meter' – that is, the enviable situation in which one's burgeon-ing reputation outstrips actual performance as a determinant of further advancement. When this happens, previous advance-ment is taken as *evidence* of suitability for further advancement up the ladder. Some kind of transformation comes over a man having once been the (e.g.) youngest ever district manager when he discovers that, not only can he, to his surprise, do it after all, but it is actually *easier* than the messy and less predict-able jobs down the line. Then, the universe opens up for him; he begins to exude luck and to attract it in greater measure. In the process, he is likely to remain quite an agreeable person; he has had to stab hardly any backs and he has no cause to fall prey to envy, that most disfiguring of sins. As a product of the patronage system he is, too, the perfect patron, bound to choose wisely. Unfortunately, luck is, to a large extent, a closed-system commodity. There isn't enough to go around, by definition, and the fortunate tend to find the disfigurement of others difficult to comprehend.

The other attraction of the Irish study was its focus on so small a community. London is a more complex city than Dublin, but still retains an air of overlapping villages, each with its squires, policemen and idiots. I have referred above to that tight network of approved industrialists who have success-fully shifted from being 'in business' to helping the nation *with* business. The City of London too always reminds me powerfully of certain inbred hamlets in Suffolk where one ought not to be too surprised by the odd garb and quaint behaviour of the denizens. The difference is that, in the City, they really can be dangerous. I don't know how many people really matter in the City but my guess would be that the number is governed by Parkinsonian considerations rather than function. How many people, in other words, does it take to sustain a power network?

The rubber spider web The existence of these networks is clearly linked with the issue of luck. If British society can be thought of as a rubber spider web (to borrow an idea from Professor Tom Lupton; if you tweak it, it shivers a bit but soon gets back to where it was) then the trick is to get as close to the centre as you possibly can. You will meet all the right people and that alone will ensure the opportunity to succeed. The same considerations apply to the media. The hero-threshold of the British press is notoriously low and, once established as a familiar figure, only a substantial scandal can remove you from its pages. For the newspapers I use the analogue of the supermarket shelf – it is the same size every day and there is only so much room next to the checkout at eye-level. The trick is to be there. The perennial problem for the journalists has been their appalling track record in picking durable heroes. Living as they do in a world of much power and no real authority, they are obsessed by power and by its proponents. Unfortunately, it is usually these same people who come spectacular croppers.

One intriguing feature of the Irish study is the odd correlation between perceived innovativeness in Irish business and religious fundamentalism. It is as if, in a country like Ireland, if you leave the creation to God, your energies may be released for creativity in other spheres. In America, the opposite tends to be the case; that is, innovativeness and philosophical turmoil go together. I mention this odd factor in the context of British business morals and, in particular, the curious historical splitting of the great Quaker companies from the hard mainstream of British business belief. One fundamental question facing the aspiring young manager must be one of morals: if you sincerely want to succeed, can it be done in complete honesty? What is the minimum number of backs to be stabbed, or scratched, backhanders to be dished out consistent with the likelihood of success? Is hard work and a reliance on the formal authority of the management development institutions going to be enough?

Defining success in big organizations The Irish study throws light on success at community level. Much the same phenomena obtain within the tight communities of the big firms. Here too the individual has to decide how closely he wishes to be drawn, or push himself, to the centre of the organizational web. Dr

Robert Rapoport illuminated this problem most helpfully in his study of some 600 managers passing through the Henley Administration Staff College. As with the Irish study he deployed a wide range of measures – psychological, sociological, historical – to arrive at a rich and subtle typology of the managers in question. In this case the typologies were more aptly described as 'career orientations', that is, ways the managers found to relate themselves to employing organizations.

The main orientations turned out to be:

1 The *metamorphic*. These are the ambitious, energetic, creative risk-taking, change-oriented managers who, if they cannot change the obstructing situation, or themselves, are likely to move on elsewhere. They get deeply involved in the organization so long as it also retains a metamorphic character, but tend to pop out like a cork under pressure when frustrated. This is, in fact, the 'spiralist' career pattern.

2 The *incremental*. These managers develop by cumulative steps along a given track or channel, tending to accept the organization as it is. They are more likely than metamorphics to adapt themselves to fit the organization. When the incremental pattern is associated with managerial competence, advancement tends to be steady and to be accompanied by considerable personal satisfaction and happiness. It is not easy to say whether the inexorable growth of the public sector in Britain is cause or effect of an increasing number of incremental types in the culture.

3 The *tangential*. These are those people who take up a position of, often creative, dissent in relation to organizations. They tend to be dissatisfied with many elements in the work environment, finding it cool, divided and excessively bureaucratic. However, given a constructive orientation and competence, the tangentials manage to cope with these feelings by gravitating towards peripheral roles where both individual and organizational needs may be served simultaneously. These are the 'gatekeepers' on the boundaries of organizational systems and sub-systems. Essentially, these are people who succeed in making their internal conflicts explicit and continuing to work with, and at them.

4 The *humanistic*. This group, predictably smaller in a management population passing through an external course, comprises people who enjoy life in the round – family, leisure and personal interests and who resist career advancement if it appears to threaten other areas of life. They are likeable, tolerant and sometimes rather dull and they rarely

rise to those positions where there is much chance of imposing their admirable values on the systems they work in.

A culture of dependent assumptions is more likely to produce types 2, 3, 4, rather than Metamorphics, the types who spoil for a challenge or a fight. If the cherished values are felt to be outside work (and felt to be insupportable *at* work) then the field is left to cautious time-servers (Incrementals), vacillating potential escapees (Tangentials), and true escapees (Humanists). Of course, something has gone seriously wrong in corporate life when the Humanists *have* to escape.

Egan's and Rapoport's work appeals to me because they both set the current make-up of the subject managers in their long-term historical context. Who you decided to marry does have a bearing on the way you take up a managerial role, whatever your management 'style', your decision-making method, or your technical expertise. Similarly, whether or not you have 'presence', or whatever that magical quality is that inspires confidence, is probably a function of career luck many years ago. I used to suggest to my middle management audiences that one of the main tricks was to maintain LPM (low peripheral movement), based on the observation that dominant leaders in the animal kingdom invariably move slowly and gravely in the *centre* of their bands, maintaining only a beady and intense eye contact with immediately subordinate males. There is no doubt that those who keep their physical cool, whilst all about are flailing around, are magnets of attention. It is in fact possible to convert the most unprepossessing of chief executives into magnets of attention by forcing them to watch themselves on television. Provided, that is, they have the capacity to convert sensory data (the sight of themselves) into motor skills (the physical control and presentation of themselves).

For all the efforts of various teachers and management developers, I suspect the capacity for serious work, for luck and for personal 'presence' are built into us from a very early age through very primitive processes. Most of us would accept, for example, that an emotionally insecure (or absent) mother would lead to emotional insecurity in children. But it is only in recent years that scientists have begun to speculate seriously about the origins of thought in the very young, even in unborn babies. Bion even suggests that if the mother is incapable, physically or psychologically, of acting as a container and converter of infantile dread and panic then the outcome might be an adult incapable of effective *thought*, because, as the brain was forging its primitive internal links, certain connections were not made at exactly the right stage of development. The breast, for example, is more than a physically satisfying milk bar, it is an *idea*. The baby's primitive preconception of a breast (a kind of breast-shaped blank in the mind), programmed into the circuitry of the brain, has to mate with the physical object for the *idea* to form and for the brain to establish that link.

This may seem a long way removed from management development, yet my guess is there is a close correlation between executives of the Survival type and those incapable of conceptual thought. Such people are usually skilled in covering up their intellectual inadequacies, mostly by frightening people; but partly also by ensuring that nothing which swims into their purview is ever longer than a page or so in length. It is called ensuring 'effective staffwork' and may even enhance a reputation for incisiveness. My experience is that such people can concentrate hard only for about thirty to forty minutes after which their eyes begin to glaze and physical activity takes over. Usually, their over-full diaries rescue them. The point is that there is a remarkable number of such people in high places in important organizations – not only bullies but essentially stupid as well. If the 'management development' people are impressed by such things, if they confuse stupidity with incisiveness, then they are defining 'management' in a special, and narrow, way.

This line of argument leads to the intriguing possibility that typical successes are of two main types:

1 The Survival type, so badgered by a sense of internal emptiness, that he cannot stop running (what makes Sammy run is what was lacking from the start). He may not be a genius, but his manic energies will ensure he 'outsurvives' everybody. The classic *entrepreneur*, as J. K. Galbraith has commented 'Like *Apis mellifera*, the male mosquito, achieves his act of

creation at the cost of his own extinction'. I offend no one; A. Mellifera will not be reading such a book as this and certainly not with a beer to hand and socks off.

2 The natural leader, with a sense of inner completeness and secure identity deriving from a life-time's experience of abundance. Such people can think very straight indeed and readily cope with the psychological projections of other people without feeling too threatened and without taking their eye off the ball (Work).

The Joe Soaps of this world, neither so strong in identity, nor so scarred by life, puddle along in the background. They aren't impressive enough to be natural leaders nor are they obsessive enough to overcome all obstacles. Meanwhile, in the stratosphere, the successes are locked in an implicit combat – good gods versus bad gods, Workers versus Survivors, givers versus takers – a combat which cuts across organizational boundaries, hierarchies and seniorities, the outcome of which will be, ultimately, our new conceptions of leadership in society. Whether 'management development', as it has evolved, has had anything to do with this epic struggle of values is doubtful. If it *hasn't*, we must ask what on earth it has been up to.

Management development as a social defence system

What then is management development *for*? The chart on p. 149 suggests the link between some of the underlying anxieties of corporate life and the particular forms of management development which act as defences against those anxieties. Here I refer to a whole body of fascinating organizational study based on those institutions with a dominant throughput of *people*. Of course, all organizational systems have people passing through them, but only organizations like airlines, hospitals, schools, seminaries, brothels and management development schemes have the processing of people as the *primary* task. Research suggests that such institutions create particular pressures on, and anxieties for, those who run them and in particular for those who have to deal, at first hand, with the throughput. It is not uncommon for women to be lumbered with the anxiety-absorbing function of such institutions as in,

Management development as a social defence system Wherever management development has surfaced as a specialism (mostly in Anglo-Saxon culture – UK, USA and the other colonies) it has acted as a social defence system. That is to say, whatever MD is *supposed* to do (training, succession planning, etc.) it *also* helps people to defend themselves against certain threats inherent in organizational life and human psychology. Some of these threats are listed in column 4 (below). Each type of threat is associated with, or gives rise to, a certain vision or model of organizational life and organizational management is reflected in a mode of 'management development' (column 2). (These 'management development' approaches are discussed in more detail on pp. 129–31.) Each of them has a different dominant throughput (what *must* be achieved if the 'management development' unit is to survive in that sort of organizational culture). Finally, all these manifestations are linked with historical precedents (column 5).

Dominant assumption definition of 'management'	Implicit assumption about 'management development'	Dominant management development throughput	Particular objects of social defence system (the fears, doubts and bogeys managers are heir to)	Historical precedents
Corporate Control	Military	Paper	Fear of chaos (usually projection of fears of internal chaos) Fear of desertion (i.e. disloyalty) Fear of insubordination	Rise of the big, complex organization Nostalgia for military victories past Binary vision of society (i.e. officers and men)
Corporate Dependence	Family	Reassurance	Doubts about legitimacy of corporate purposes Fear of capricious use of power Fear of non-recognition as an individual and of independence	Revulsion from excesses of industrial past Rise of the big organization Development of a national culture of dependence
Corporate Growth	Educational	'Motivation'	Doubts about legitimacy of corporate purposes (civilizing and ceremonializing versions) Humble social origins (civilizing and ceremonializing versions) Fear of career death and of death itself (updating version)	Cultural trust in 'education' as a value especially education based on formal curricula Traditional low status of industry Massive borrowing of American 'management' assumptions (absent leadership)

for example, the work of airline stewardesses, nurses and course registrars. Meanwhile, the pilots, the surgeons and the professors maintain a discreet and manageable distance from the more sordid aspects of the human beings in process.

In fact, the management educational institutions manage this particular trick in a complementary way to the hospitals. If you are hospitalized, you are expected to, as it were, hang up your brain at the door and leave your body to the doctors, If you show signs of taking an intelligent interest in your case, they have ways of making you feel both neurotic and hypo-chondriacal. Conversely, in the management school, you hang up your guts at the door and bring in just the brain. If you can't separate the two, there is always the registrar to weep with you and, if necessary, hospitalize you. Management develop-ment and management education don't employ many women

The splitting of human beings for processing:

	Hang up at the door	Bring in for Processing
1. Hospital	Brains	Guts
2. Management Education	Guts	Brains

so far, mostly, I suspect, because such institutions are captured in rational/logical/decision-making assumptions about manage-ment work and everybody knows women can't think straight – too 'emotional'.

The real problem with women, and those who boast feminine sensibilities, is their capacity to feel compassion and to detect humbug. If much of the management development edifice built up since the war represents in reality a large shock-absorber to soak up some of the pressures of mid-career frustra-tion and of mid-life depression, then a nose for humbug and a sense of compassion are probably disqualifiers for the job. Such qualities might lead you to think that mid-career and mid-life are periods that people ought to be able to manage for themselves, including non-managers. You might even think that, at the conjunction of corporate purpose and individual life, there *ought* to be a few shocks transmitted in both directions so we do not delude ourselves about what corporate life does to people and what, in a variety of covert ways, the people manage to do back.

In fact, I am misusing the physics of the shock-absorber here. If it is working properly, a shock-absorber does not absorb all the shock, but transmits some of it back into the sub-frame, in a modified form. That might be a workable description of an effective management development role – tightly tensioned (and heavy duty) shock-absorber for middle management stress; a role, and a person to match, capable of acknowledging the existence of shock, but able to receive, modify and feed it back to source in such a way that it can be dealt with realistically and constructively. At risk of overstretching the metaphor, current models of management development are tuned wrongly; the family model, for example, akin to the springing system of one of those vast wallowing American saloons and the military and educational models more like a certain brutal British sports car where you can insert chocks of wood in the suspension in order to eradicate springing altogether. The trick, as in most things, is to find a proper balance.

Management development and evil

I have suggested that little of use can be learned by observing separately *either* the formal systems by which organizations staff themselves in order to survive and prosper *or* the power networks which develop around those formal systems. All organizations have a formal and informal system coexisting and any understanding is going to derive from an inspection of their constant interaction. Furthermore, my experience of organizations is that they tend to arrive at some kind of equilibrium between those who, for the most part, get on with the job and those who are, for the most part, absorbed with 'getting on'.

The former group have, on balance, a valency for Work, the substance of an organization, the latter, on balance, a valency for Survival. No doubt, such valencies are built-in for many people but I am suggesting here that Work and Survival themselves establish an organizational equilibrium which must then be related to by the people. (Palmer and Reed.)

The management development professional always has to position himself in relation to the formal and informal subsystems, standing outside of them in order to help run one of them with a weather eye on the other. I worked in one company for a period where the Survival types in higher management were known, almost affectionately, as 'the rat pack'. Part of my job, it seemed to me, was to engage in periodical lunches of what seemed to me almost mind-bending insincerity with members of the pack. Insincerity is probably, technically, the wrong word because my impression is that both parties usually had no illusions whatsoever about where the other stood; it is only when one party gets the wrong end of the stick, e.g. Chamberlain/Hitler, that such arrangements seize up.

Discussion along these lines leads quickly to the notion that management development stands at the centre of a struggle between good and evil, and so it often seems to management development people, standing as they do for equitable treatment for everybody in relation to work and talent. The key word is *work*. Too often, the formal management development institutions are fought for simply because they *are* formal and hence neater and more easily controllable. Too often, the informal is deplored simply because it *is* informal; it breaks the rules, is furtive and elusive. But the real justification for the formal is that it is more closely associated with the *work* system than the informal, precisely because the rat packs of this world concentrate on work only when it appears to suit their career interests. They do not, as do the true Workers, become absorbed in the intrinsic purposes of the work.

The formal system is therefore authorized by *everybody* (everybody, that is, who feels in tune with the organization's work) because organizational survival depends on work. I have to say, however, that my rat pack luncheons were nearly always funnier, more engaging, more intuitive and revealing than any proper meetings around the formal system. If the rat pack has anything (what makes Sammy run) it has *energy* and when that energy is bent to work great things may happen. Many sales managers for example argue that salesmen operate best when slightly frightened. That may be largely true for Survival types; it is a less attractive trait when the salesmen move up amongst the management fat cats (to draw on an alternative expression used in the same company) where the Survival manager may wreak havoc by sustaining his characteristic level of fear, Fight, and Flight at their familiar thresholds.

The point about rat pack energy is that it will not be disciplined to organizational rat runs. If survival is your dominant mode, you will survive *despite* the system. Indeed, if survival is your mode; your experience of life has probably led you to a conviction that the system is out to get you unless you are mighty quick. For management development, the task is not to control the rat pack; it can't be done; but to try to understand them and, from time to time, bend their energies in the direction of work. But, accept from the start, they will always outrun you, in the sense that a man in mortal danger (real or imaginary) has the strength and endurance of ten men.

There is a risk, I think, in talking of rat packs that I may be interpreted as thinking only of trade and commerce and of big organizations at that. I have in mind every local government bureaucracy, hospital, professional group, university (*particularly* university) and voluntary organization that I have ever seen. The tendency towards Work or Survival is in us all, but it is skewed very differently from person to person. Returning to the theme of good and evil, it is relatively easy, on entering an organization for the first time, to distinguish between:

1 Those people who can be relied upon to concentrate on substantive issues of moment and to lose themselves in their intrinsic significance; and,
2 Those people whose eyes begin to dart about nervously after a while because they can't see what the discussion will contribute to their own survival and, worse, it shows some likelihood of illuminating their own power position too clearly, like someone suddenly caught in a spotlight.

The work/survival continuum

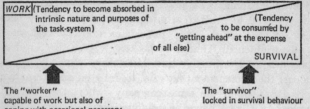

The "worker"
capable of work but also of
coping with occasional necessary
forays into survival behaviour

The "survivor"
locked in survival behaviour

Although some people may remain relatively fixed on the continuum, especially chronic survival-types, others may move backwards and forwards along it, in a recurring wave pattern. Indeed, it has been argued that the highest peaks of work creativity (in artistic endeavour, for example) are commonly preceded by a trough of despondency as the enormity of the projected work threatens to engulf the individual – *threatens* to engulf because it *is* possible to go on working at an external task whilst keeping in touch with one's inner world of fantasy, gods and demons, panic. The true worker continuously seeks to extend his work, passing in each stage to a higher and more demanding plane with all the accompanying fears of failure and of being overwhelmed by events. If he has coped with Survival in mid-life, he can, in all likelihood, cope with these recurrent and unavoidable crises in Work.

Most organizations seem, somehow, to contain approximately equal numbers of each sort of character. However, there are examples of organizations, including countries, tipping over completely to the bully-boys. When that is in danger of happening, it is probably no bad thing for individuals to think in terms of good and evil so as to mobilize enough Fight to restore the balance. I doubt an organization could ever tip the other way because fears for survival are such a consistent part of the human make-up and the Survival types, unlike some of us, never stop running.

Returning to the meaning of the phrase 'management development', it appears to contain within it the latent tension between work (corporate purposes) and survival (individual purposes). In Survival mode, you are on your own; in work, you are bound, with others, through a structure of roles, to achieve something.

Thus: *management = corporate work*
       development = individual survival

Management development is not supposed to mean precisely this, but this can, nonetheless, be seen as an implicit, operating definition for many people. Furthermore, in Britain, the career progression aspect of management development has tended to dominate the specialism as evidenced by the prevalent internal models of operation; the army, the school and the family. These are institutions for which we rarely seek a fundamental purpose or output; they *exist*, notionally for 'defence', 'education' and maturation of the young, but also because they have always provided frameworks within which people are enabled to move from one point of their lives to another, just as the Church has provided a structure and an explanation for the passage from birth to death.

Of course, I am not contesting the need for these structures, nor complaining that management development has, since the war, supplied them in relation to careers. Rather, I am worried about *work* and about the way in which the very idea of 'management' (that is, Management II as defined in Chapter 1) has become split-off from the idea of work, so that people who worship at the right shrines ('management education') and scratch the right backs may often rise in the ranks of management without ever demonstrating the guts and the wits necessary to get really important things done. Management development has always therefore been about legitimacy, but often of a shallow and bogus kind. The only legitimacy that matters in the end is the output the organization is meant to generate and that means work.

For the English in particular, the very idea of 'work' has become split off from *outputs* and hence from realistic achievement. 'Work' is, rather, a pastime – a means of extending the individual's human relationships; the matter of outputs and hence justification is assumed to be taken care of by somebody else, somewhere else; higher up. In that setting, 'management' and 'management development' become associated with Dependence rather than with the sort of fight you automatically get into when you set out to achieve something.

Using the Work/Survival continuum one can construct a whole series of overlapping relationships between the two sub-populations of an enterprise. Again I stress that everybody is both a Worker and a Survivor, but we skew in different directions, or towards different poles.

	The workers	*The survivors*
Natural terrain:	Authority structure	Power network
Modus operandi:	Role	Personal Contact
Dominant output:	Products/services	Personal success
World view:	Consensus	Conflict
Emotional patterning:	Mature dependence	Fight/Flight
Infantile experience:	Love, abundance, Dependence and parental containment and amelioration of fear	Frigidity, emotional withholding, inconsistent Dependence and the rejection of infantile fears
Encounter with the mid-life period:	Confrontation and resolution	Manic defence

In thinking about the Survivors (I am thinking about the 'survival' emotional patterning here; by no means all the Survival types in fact survive) I revert once again to Bion and the first few weeks of life. I have drawn considerable succour from the thought, when once again I have been outrun and outfoxed by a classical power figure, that, many years ago, the breast was withheld from him, or his parents had read those books that advised leaving babies to cry for twenty minutes till they stopped, or his poor mother knew not how to provide dependence and to soak up panic. The thought has not helped me much directly either as consultant or manager but I find it has a curiously soothing effect under stress and that, in itself, may be helpful in absorbing some of the latent panic of the frightened survivor types with whom I have to deal sometimes.

It is easy, if you happen to hold a consensus world view, to look at the above list in terms of good and evil. I certainly find it easy, in the company of leaden, determined and small-minded machine politicians to smell evil in the air. More to the point, those in the lower ranks can smell it too, which is why industrial relations troubles stubbornly resist 'logical' solutions. When we look back at the post-war years with the wisdom of historical perspective we are bound to be amazed how it was that disembodied *quantities* of all kinds, particularly quantities of money, drove out our appreciation of the *qualities* we still (especially our women) understood in our guts. 'Management By Objectives' in particular was an extraordinary denial of several thousand years of accumulated learning about the *quality* of working relationships. Reducing work to the measurable (and, presumably, unarguable) took the Fight out of it as well as such useful, but unmeasurable, notions as leadership, integrity, sensitivity, insight, judgement, common sense and so on – *good* qualities, on the whole. The machine politicians, the Survivors, don't have an in-built detector for good and evil, manifested in themselves or in others. Their sensory antennae operate along other, oblique dimensions. Indeed, one can imagine the awkward and discomfited reaction of survival types to my introduction here of such ideas at all. My guess is that good and evil, or some more fashionable surrogate words will soon be finding their way back into the language if only to grapple with corruption on the sort of scale we now increasingly find it in public and private life. I am not thinking of corruption simply in terms of cooking the books but rather the insidious corruption, inside the person, arising from too much time spent in a power network engaged in 'Mickey Mouse' purposes.

After twenty-five years, the fundamental failures of management development have been threefold:

1 The failure to recognize that 'management' was, in the first place, a bizarre, culture-bound (British, American and British colonial), insecure concept upon which to build a movement and a specialism.

2 The failure to see that if management development was about anything, it was about helping *all* the people to relate their own life systems to the corporate career and task system and to fight about it, if need be.

3 The failure to see that management development, thus defined, was a moral issue.

To put it another way, most of the practitioners really believe they know what 'management' means, can't think in systems terms, especially about life itself and imagine that they deal primarily in numbers – enough people recorded or trained; enough forms filled in etc. I have spent many years in the trade and plead guilty to all of it. What to do? Such fundamental issues are largely non-delegable. The failure of management development has been also the failure of chief executives to recognize the centrality of these matters. If management development means holding people in suspension, processing them, reassuring them, 'motivating' them to carry on despite the ennui brought on by aimless bureaucratic in-fighting, it must mean that the executive system has failed to provide sound and responsive structures for work. In such a structure designed for work, where top people keep their eye on the ball and inspire by example, 'management development' ought, for the most part, to look after itself.

8 Management education

Across the wall, in the verdant pastures of academia, the counterpart to 'management development' was 'management education'. It too saw quick growth in the years following World War II; rather quicker, in fact, than the industrial and commercial sector it was meant to stimulate. I mentioned before that the Continental Europeans have managed with rather less of this particular commodity although it seems to have done them little harm. What they do have in abundance is educational institutions designed to prepare people for *doing* certain kinds of work and, what's more, they are institutions of high status. What Britain has is a small network of extremely powerful educational institutions which, while providing some guidance about doing, preponderantly teach how to *be* a certain kind of person. It has always been true of Oxbridge, and it was probably expecting too much of the new management education Establishment that it would entirely avoid the same trap – that is, becoming dominated by acculturization for social roles at the expense of work itself.

The origins of British management education are deeply rooted in British Binary Thinking. Since 1946 there had been Henley, the archetypal country house, modelled on the very big companies' similar establishments. The head of one of those establishments once reflected to me, 'We are really in the civilizing business here', as though the sons of toil he dealt with were Hottentots fresh off the veldt. But when the 'white heat' era came in the late fifties and early sixties and real money began to be spent on management education, the obvious influences were Harvard, MIT and urban America rather than pastoral Britain. Indeed, Henley had always prided itself, with some justification, on its 'pastoral' provision for the middle level manager in need of time to think. On the other hand, London and Manchester were the outcomes of an argument, and a traditional one at that, around the old north/south split; should the business schools' primary task be to spend a longish time nurturing a 'seedcorn' (note the agricultural analogue again) of bright young men for a brighter future, or should they quickly get to work on the old lags who, like it or not, were in charge of ailing manufacturing enterprises up and down the country, mostly up? Not surprisingly, it was the hard men from the Midlands espousing the latter view. Whatever the outcome, it was assumed at the time that what came to pass would be unequivocally about *doing* and, more important, doing in the key jobs.

But the British social structure is not outflanked so easily. Ten years later almost the most important man in the London

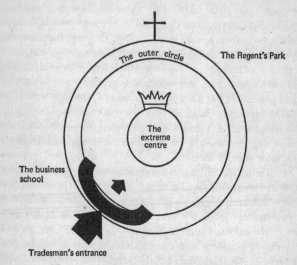

The outer circle

The Regent's Park

The extreme centre

The business school

Tradesman's entrance

Management education as the re-entry to the culture of dependence from the despised outskirts of trade (symbolised by John Nash's Regents Park)

Business School remains John Nash, the creator of its magnificent home. You enter the place round the back, nearest the noise and hubbub of urban London, walking into a humdrum, convex modern shell. A few paces east (or, symbolically, six to ten weeks or one to two years later) you emerge cradled by the concave Palladian splendour of the old front, into the Regent's Park. 'Here', it was said, is 'every man a king!' The sensation is more than symbolic; if you happen to work in despised industry and, worse, if you missed university of any kind, not to mention Oxbridge, then to pass through this building is to press a little closer to the extreme centre of concentric British society. It is not a process to be despised; it is a matter of no little import to British businessmen to be made whole again, to re-enter society more fully from the social outskirts of trade and commerce.

The movement of managers into, through and out of management education institutions is a rich and paradoxical process. On the one hand, the manager is re-entering the traditional, not to say stuffy, university world – a world, it is supposed, of continuity, old and cherished standards, disinterested enquiry, a rigorous pursuit of truth more or less uninterrupted since Socrates. That is precisely what the average manager likes about management education and what he craves from it.

But, as it happens, the average industrial manager is often a much more strait-laced character than the tutors he is likely to encounter in the world of management education – much more likely to have remained loyal to a single employer, more likely to have soldiered on with wife Number 1, much less likely to have experimented with different life-styles. He is unlikely to have managed his 'career' as cleverly as his professors, but he may well understand the diagram on p. 118 better than they and to place a higher value on old-fashioned authority. At a management school, he is torn between the desire to tune into a slick, dispassionate, number-crunching form of expertise – all cool decision-making and not much sentiment – and, on the other hand, a desire to luxuriate in Dependent and reflective surroundings and to muse on higher things in the way university students are supposed to.

I used the example of the London Business School above because its setting is so old and beautiful. But all management education is bedevilled thus. Dedicated management teachers who wish to get down to basics with their students find they are presiding over rituals of a semi-religious kind, for many of their students anyway. My own researches on this subject indicate that the only students prepared to *fight* for their rights in this setting are those middle-class graduates who are unimpressed by the socialization element in management education and prepared to go back to the course brochure as their source of authority. Not all observers of the scene might agree with my stress, in Chapter 5, on *production* (outputs) as the ultimate source of managerial authority and identity. Many would have to agree, however, that a close identification with the production process has *not* been the central issue in management education (it is indeed difficult to get those in the manufacturing function on to courses at all). Rather, management has tended to be approached as a series of disembodied skills or techniques rather than as a central and linking *point of view* about the world.

At about the time the business schools were establishing themselves, there were very few names of any real distinction on the management education front in Britain – indeed anywhere. In the USA, Russell Ackoff was already institutionalizing methods by which managers on normal courses took responsibility for tutoring their colleagues in their own areas of specialization. The two European giants, in their different ways, were probably the late Dr A. K. Rice and Professor R. W. Revans because, for all the theoretical talk that was going on, they were *operationalizing*, after the fashion of managers, completely new designs for managerial learning, which respected the integrity and the mental constructs of the managers themselves but at the same time made some progress towards a theory of managerial learning and application. Above all, they had devised methods which elevated the discourse above mere techniques and which called upon managers to examine what they were really up to in their work.

The crucial link between Rice's 'Working Conferences' on authority at the Tavistock Institute and Revans's exchange programmes of executives in hospitals (in Britain) and commercial enterprises (in Belgium) was that the managers concerned were assumed to have a great deal of wisdom to share with each other, provided that a helpful setting for doing so could be provided. Revans did it by concrete, managerial project work in an organization other than one's own; Rice and his colleagues took an existing Tavistock model for the study of 'group relations', *per se*, and converted it to a means for studying *authority*. The notable absentee from both models was the 'expert' with a 'subject' upon which to 'lecture'. Revans and Rice were forcing managers to face up to the essentially divergent nature of their work and their wisdom about it and, in order to do it, casting the convergers out of the temple (see Chapter 10). This version of events is an unfamiliar one within the schools, where different sorts of giants were being manufactured. Rice, part of a separate tradition based on the Tavistock Institute, remained split-off from 'management education' and from all but a minority of big organizations in the same way as numerous important innovators had before him.

Revans was however closer to home. The Tavistock is often associated in the industrial mind with the subconscious and thence, rather illogically, with illness and therapy. However, Revens at that time was based in the Manchester Institute of Science and Technology and was thus, geographically and technically, uncomfortably close to the heartland of British management. His ultimate departure to Brussels, and points east, was in some ways symptomatic of the state of thinking in British management education in the 1960s. The clarity and simplicity of his insight was intolerable. What he said, for all its directness, was truly incomprehensible to those who had already elevated the process of running things properly to the level of a proper object of academical study. Equally, Revans could not understand what the new priesthood of management education was saying:

I am well aware that I do not share many of the present values of the academic world. My insistence that the first need of any science, namely *that one should continuously observe its field of action at first hand* – that we should involve the managers themselves in collecting and interpreting the data necessary for successful decision-making – has been dismissed as unscientific, as poor research, and as unlikely to lead to any understanding of management, either as art or as science. I cannot reply to these arguments, simply because I do not understand them. I shall, however, cheerfully bear the reproach of conspiring to adulterate the standards of university scholarship. I conclude with a quotation from Hazlitt's essay *On the Ignorance of the Learned*: 'Learning is, in too many cases . . . a substitute for true knowledge. Books are less often made use of as spectacles to look at nature with, than as blinds to keep out its strong light and shifting scenery from weak eyes and indolent dispositions . . . The most sensible people to be met with in society are men of business and of the world, who argue from what they see and know, instead of spinning cobweb distinctions of what things ought to be.'

Perhaps it is significant that both Revans's and Rice's most important founding experiences of managerial learning at work occurred with ordinary working people in, respectively, Nigeria and India (Revans, 1971; Rice, 1958.) There, the managerial task is as forbidding as anywhere else in the world, but the approach is more direct and less trammelled with text-book wisdom and techniques. Rice's 'Working Conferences' have spread all over the world and so too now have Revans's 'action learning' programmes. In Britain, very few executives of significant organizations have heard of either of them.

The hot potato If we look closely at what 'management development' has been up to over twenty years and, more importantly, what it has chosen to ignore, we can make more sense of the business schools' and university management departments' phenomenological roles. What, in other words, have the big corporations been exporting to the business schools and what kinds of pay-offs have they been getting back to encourage them to go on with it? Incredibly, there remain a great many people, in and outside the schools, who feel the curriculum to be the centre of the universe. What doubts exist are alleviated by a steady flow of funds into 'evaluation research' which purports to explicate the process of filling half-empty receptacles with new knowledge and measuring how much is then poured back into sponsoring organizations.

Of course, it occasionally happens that a particular man, with a particular want of particular knowledge, defines his work role in such a way that the application of that knowledge captures his attention from the start. But, it is a relatively rare event; as it must be when the schools have to cater for so many people from such diverse working situations. Evaluation research depends on a network of assumptions; that 'management' can be defined satisfactorily as an activity in the first place and that a particular aspect of measurable learning may be linked with a specific management act back on the job. Further, it depends upon making a judgement that such a management act is necessarily 'better' or 'worse' than a score of other, qualitatively different, management acts which might have been perpetrated. At base, the wish, amongst the more unregenerate sections of management education, is to believe that management knowledge can be codified, carried away and applied, like so much paste, to the world of real problems.

There is no evidence that it is so, which means we must seek elsewhere for an explanation of the survival of management education in its present forms. Here, the management development professionals in the big firms are often wiser than those they represent and many of those from whom they buy. For them, management education is primarily about acculturization, about providing an opportunity for young or rough-at-the-edges managers to learn how to comport themselves in high places. Management students rarely apply anything of substantive usefulness but they almost invariably return more *confident* from the experience. What that confidence is a function *of* is difficult to determine, but its importance ought not to be underestimated. I am certainly not suggesting that it is a negligible output of such expenditure. With a few exceptions, even the managers-at-a-plateau, who are promotable nowhere, but still sent away for management education, experience a boost in confidence sufficient, perhaps, to carry them through to near-retirement.

There was a good joke which appeared in the London *Financial Times* some years ago about a fantasy management education establishment with no faculty. Participants, on arrival, were greeted by an automatically-activated tape recorder message to this effect:

Good evening gentlemen, welcome to the X management education establishment. You will have noted, perhaps with relief, the absence of faculty or curriculum. This is a regular feature of this programme and a closely-guarded secret of its alumni, present and past. If you should require any inducement to keep this secret you may be influenced by the £500 in crisp ten-pound notes which is to be found in a brown envelope in your bedroom. This represents half the fee paid by your employers and approximates expenditure that would otherwise have been incurred with respect to teaching staff salaries and related costs. In the meantime, meals and other services will be provided and the bar will remain open at normal opening times. You will have discovered that your colleagues are drawn from similar organizations to your own and contain amongst them a wealth of practical experience in all manner of managerial roles. There is also a first-rate library at your disposal. How you decide to pass these six weeks is your own managerial decision; we trust you will enjoy it and find it beneficial. Thank you.

Like all good jokes, it doesn't stretch credulity too far. The fundamental truth expressed is the reality that middle managers on courses have much more in common with each other's predicaments than they have with their own employing organizations. The identity of hierarchical middleness is potentially more powerful than the identity of an ICI man versus a Ford man or whatever. Too often, this is denied by the middle manager in his hope, or fantasy, that he is one of the minority of participants with a field marshall's baton in his knapsack; that he may soon become *Mister* ICI or *Mister* Ford. Normal management education subsists on the collective fantasy, entertained most hysterically by post-graduate students, that *all* will ascend to the heights. Managers, even relatively successful ones, are not allowed to brood about relative career failure. Managers, in short, are not supposed to be depressed.

I have suggested a range of phenomenal tasks for management education, all of them to do with acculturization, socialization and the reinforcement of confidence. But what lies behind the edifice; would sponsors continue to pay out for the commodity if that was all it was? Of course, it helps to believe in the efficacy of the curriculum but few do, in business at least; the talk is rather of 'rubbing shoulders', 'making contact', 'seeing how the world works', 'broadening' and other such sophisticated concepts. More convincing explanations are to be found in the incapacity of big organizations to construct a logic of career progression with any convincing connection with legitimacy – either the legitimacy of the organization's purposes and the competence to pursue them or the legitimacy of the individual employee in the role of citizen.

Instead, the individual usually gives himself to the organization, dependently, as a child, and relinquishes at work any direct concern with his personal value system. In entering what is essentially a power system he gives up autonomy. He expects to get ahead, if at all, on who he knows and his relationship with the fundamental purposes of the firm is usually no closer than the very moral gentlemen (Chapter 5) who made expensive, mostly-air bread without thinking it odd at all. Without the discipline of an identifiable client and without the conviction that old fashioned standards really count for anything at work, he is caught, and badly caught.

In response, the corporation (that is, those able and lucky enough to have 'made it' already) supplies a 'management development' programme. The great mass of the managers, kept going on a diet of hope until just too old to break out, are usually not well-equipped to face up to the questioning of the mid-life period; to face what is involved in:

1. Managing one's own career realistically, and
2. Coming to terms, in the latter half of one's working life, with one's internal value system.

How do you give autonomy back to managers; autonomy to manage their lives efficiently via legitimate work roles? It isn't an easy matter:

Many of the same managers have little trust in the first place in the legitimacy of trade and business – a historical legacy.

Many are dependent before ever they sign on, a product of society at large.

Organizational size, of which these are partial symptoms, is a relatively new phenomenon of industrial history. People are not used to being caught in the middle or dealing with the phenomenon from the top.

Middle managers have already adopted defensive, Survival modes of habitual behaviour, projecting their conflicts into subordinates and top management. They are, therefore, powerfully defended against serious examination of the most important problems facing them.

It isn't easy to restore managerial autonomy but it is important, otherwise management education will continue to be misused for a variety of unacknowledged tasks:

Helping to deny the manager's growing awareness of mortality.

Providing a bogus form of legitimacy, largely unconnected with the essential identity and purposes of the firm and the work roles which constitute it.

Sustaining the fantasy that all will inherit (in this sense, people sent away on courses represent a source of vicarious hope for those in waiting).

Supporting the pernicious fantasy that good management is mostly rational/logical decision-making and hardly leadership and trusteeship at all.

I suggest therefore that organizations, and particularly the large ones who tend to use external management education, are confronted by quite new problems of relating career structures (i.e. lives) to task structures. The problems are new because nowadays people think rather differently about the purpose of life than they used to. In the absence of belief in a central Church, meaning is increasingly sought in life itself, rather than being left for the after life. Many people find themselves, while pursuing a frankly materialist course, deeply disturbed about economic inequities within society and between societies. The issues are the same all over the developed world but, it can be argued, only in Britain does the distrust of large organizations in pursuit of profit run so deep. Thus Work itself may be without meaning in a special way in Britain, unless one can get into those callings felt to be somehow in the national interest, hardly any of which contribute to the balance of payments.

To the extent that the corporate world simply passes these issues to the management education world for partial resolution, it ducks the issue and lands the schools with what amounts to a huge dump of unprocessed dependence. To the

extent that management education has not understood the process, has developed hardly any workable theory about it, it has fallen short of real academic respectability. Misdirected criticism of management education has been aimed at its failure to grapple, in a *counselling* way, with the personal problems of managers passing through. That is a matter for resolution between the man and the company and it is largely a question of determining a work *role* which represents a useful and fair position between the interests of both. Criticism, if any, of the management education Establishment, ought to be directed at its failures of understanding the very processes in which it is engaged. Unfortunately, these processes cannot be understood fully from the rational/logical standpoint. The same criticisms can be levelled at most university institutions but it *shows* more in the management field, because of a residual assumption that management education is about actually doing things better, whereas 'education' as a general value is something else again.

The management education establishment serves one more unacknowledged function, in this case for the company management developers and personnel people, a function which helps to explain the lasting popularity of the external course. In the complementary snobberies of industry and academia, management development professionals are no more businessmen than management education programme directors are academics. You post at the boundary someone you think can handle the relevant environment, someone who looks the part. The management developers may be engaged in entirely collusive activities on behalf of the corporation (helping to hold managers in hopeful suspension till it is too late for them to break out), but they usually *believe* themselves to be in the individual development business, almost as if their work was part of the university tradition. To sustain that illusion, the external academic institution is a godsend; possibly the best 'proof' that management development is really about chaps, rather than about sustaining the corporate system.

Everyone approves of management education, for a plethora of quite different, sometimes conflicting, reasons. Put differently, this is a system from which everybody gets a pay-off; a game in which no one, in the short term anyway, loses. Thus, it has a high survival potential; indefinitely. In the meantime, in Britain, the home of 'management' and the principal user of management education in Europe, productivity and job satisfaction are abysmally low in too many places; the managers are dispirited, confused and largely clueless about the sources of their authority, the white-collar unions are growing apace and there is no reason to imagine that unemployment will decline, ever again. So long as 'management' means something other than running things properly, we will continue to see a huge definitional gap between 'management education' and what is going wrong in the developed economies.

We see, in other words, a crisis of leadership and authority in all kinds of institutions – commercial, governmental, educational, professional and in communities and families. Part of the difficulty is that leaders bring all of themselves to work – values, prejudices and fears – in exactly the same way as ordinary workers do. Until management education, or whatever we choose to call it, deals with the whole man or woman instead of, in fantasy, the spiritless, intellectual, split-off bit that goes to the office, or the works, then it is simply toying with the core problems that face us. That is why I applaud Revans's 'Action Learning' and Reed's 'Organizational Role Analysis' (Chapter 10). They attempt to get to grips with the whole man, values and all, but in a *work* context; not in a way which invades privacy. The (binary) fantasy in management education seems to be that once you get beyond the rational/logical you are deep into psychotherapy. It just isn't so.

9 The case for a national neurosis

I suggested in Chapter 3 that the state of Britain is a cautionary tale for other developed economies. That did *not* mean 'watch out, or it might happen to you!' In my view, it *will* happen elsewhere and I can think of few, if any, countries with so stable a social and constitutional base as Britain to withstand the shocks that are coming. I take the view that the 'English disease' is not terminal cancer after all, more likely psychological in origin – a neurosis perhaps, with powerful schizoid undertones. A journalist coined the term 'euphobia' to describe the manic swings of mood Britain has enjoyed (?) in recent years. Either everything is going to be all right after all (the new oil strike, freak positive trade balances) or we are all doomed. The truth is there is a huge reservoir of calm, common sense and resilience to draw upon (well worthy of study by foreigners). But there are also matters that ought to be attended to. For example, it is *bad* for people to do anything less well than it might be done – bad for the soul. That is a quite separate consideration from shorter working weeks, loss of enthusiasm for the work ethic, anti-materialism . . . and economics generally.

As Bernard Nossiter points out, we have already heard a decade of doom-saying on the fate of Britain – Lord Robens (chairman of Vickers, a maker of arms, amongst other things): 'We are almost at the stage of the Weimar Republic before Hitler'; or Milton Friedman, the Nobel laureate economist: 'If you want an example for Britain that is highly relevant, the experience of Chile with, first, Allende and then the takeover by a military junta, is an extremely pertinent experience.'

On the subject of Britain, I try very hard to avoid the euphobic swings of mood; to hold on to some kind of middle-ground. Nossiter's book is called *Britain – A Future that Works*, and a useful antidote it is too to Robens, Friedman and all the others. I would have had to subtitle the book 'A Future that Works Tolerably Well in the Circumstances, Because Soundly Based in a Democratic/Constitutional Tradition, but Requiring All Sorts of Attention to Detail Just the Same' – not exactly an eye-catcher as a subtitle, but nearer the true mark than Nossiter's I think.

Let us review the evidence:

1 I began by introducing the notion of Binary Thought – that curiously split perspective on the world which drives out the messy, overlapping complexities in the middle and pushes all discourse to the poles. Split thinking is not the prerogative of the English, but so striking are its examples throughout history that it may be considered something of a national speciality. This is not a 'scientific' notion but a hunch. I began with the sixteenth century and Drake and the establishment of a principle that, under certain circumstances, crookedry is not really crookedry at all, provided that the joining fee for official respectability can be drummed up. I am not strong enough on British history to trace this theme further back, though one ought to note the entirely, as it were, pragmatic approach to the ultimate authority of God and his then official and wealthy representatives adopted by Henry VIII and some of his predecessors. Interestingly, the word pragmatic itself first entered the language in the sixteenth century, meaning both (i) a state decree and (ii) an agent or man of business. Initially, the *usefulness* of Binary Thought was to provide a means of preserving ideals of faith and probity whilst continuing to get very rich indeed.

2 The seventeenth and eighteenth centuries must then be seen as straightforward continuations of this theme. High principles on the one hand and on the other the successive economic rape of the colonies, the small farmers at home and, latterly, the new employees *en masse*. By now, the East India Company had taken over where Drake left off and the idea of an 'administrator' had effectively split off from the agent/ 'manager'.

3 At the beginning of the nineteenth century, Robert Owen had a good, *integrative*, idea: you could treat people decently and still make a lot of money; what's more he proved it at his Lanarkshire cotton factory. For a while, the idea seemed to catch on; his factory was visited by the Grand Duke Nicholas, soon to be Tsar, and he was befriended by the Duke of Kent. But, ultimately, Owen and his ilk were insupportable within the

tenets of Binary Thought. They got him in the end on his unorthodox religous ideas which were hostile to official Christianity. He eventually sank most of his capital in a similar project in the USA. Other organizations followed his ideas and, significantly, most are still household names, but they remained a split-off, aberrant element in the broad development of British trade and industry. It is a powerful brand of illogic which discredits so 'Christian' a man as Owen on religious grounds. Later, the same illogic was to bend even Darwin's findings to the phoney conclusion that might is right because 'science' says so.

It is easy to reflect that most of the nineteenth-century employers were both greedy and extremely stupid (which is doubtless true) but the extraordinary depths of that 'stupidity' suggest a kind of collective neurosis – a subconscious determination to blot out large chunks of reality. By the end of the century, that psychopathology was beginning to pay off in the steady decline of British manufacturing competitiveness. The Germans, meanwhile, had decided, unlike the British, that the new science was a logical element in a 'good' education. In hindsight, Owen, often described as the first socialist and, integrating as he did capitalism and decent Christian behaviour, would seem to be part of the same broad stream which brought the trade unions to respectability in 1824. However, he was *not* and we should not be surprised when we see the deep suspicion with which 'industrial democracy' has been approached by the unions since World War II.

4 The twentieth century I have described mostly in terms of collective assumptions of Dependence. It is an odd thing to say about a century containing two world wars but those now-empty victories seem to have served to kill off Fight completely, except along entirely predictable and sterile class lines – simple binary thought in the form of 'them' and 'us'. I have suggested the late A. K. Rice as the prophet for our times – 'Fight is not a problem in itself; the problem is to ensure that the fights occur between the right people, at the right time, and about the right issues.' My depiction of Britain since the turn of the century is therefore of a nation with the capacity to mobilize Fight except in the binary mode and from a Survival position. The world war is recollected with nostalgia because people were seen to be psychologically *better* then; more whole, more able apparently to mobilize effectively all their parts – Dependence, Fight/Flight or whatever, in the prosecution of a shared task.

The great puzzle must remain the ten years 1945–55. Somehow, in other European countries, latent Fight was redirected into world trade where it belongs if there doesn't happen to be a war on. There also, complex social-democratic forms of government developed, capable of tolerating the inevitable complexities and ambiguities that go with coalitions of interest. The Mother of Parliaments continued to operate as a form of microscopic sports stadium. In Britain, a nostalgic military form of industrial leadership prevailed, essentially dependent and largely clueless about the realistic role and task systems of the 'other ranks'. If you wanted *change* (which is when the fights always start) well, the Americans knew all about that. In Government, behaviour reflected an enduring, but ludicrous belief in Britain's 'world role' – *Flight*, probably, from home truth.

Thus, I have characterized England as a feminine culture, worshipping, as it were, female gods. As such, it owes nothing to Women's Lib, because it denies the relevance of the *useful* masculine traits – aggression, competitiveness, heroism and projects them either into a fantasy absent form of leadership, usually American, or into the industrial sub-culture which is then denied its useful feminine traits – such as compassion, intuition, perseverance.

Pathology and psychopathology

It is only in recent years that Britain has officially declared herself a cot case with industrial performance the principal symptom. The 'problem', as I have suggested before, is one of diagnosis. I am loath to adopt the medical analogy, firstly because there are too many doctors clustered round the patient already and secondly because it means taking up the detached, dependable, respectable posture that so often degenerates to smugness in the British 'professional' classes. My defence is that, having worked in industry for much of my life, some of it literally at the rock face, I bear some scars from whatever the ailment is.

The diagnoses have varied over time. In the immediate post-war years, the ailment didn't appear to be lethal at all. The diagnosis, if anything, was malingering. Bevan, for example, was simply puzzled that the cooperative spirit of the war years did not spill over into post-war industrial relations. By the mid-1950s, the diagnosis was nearer to one of industrial illiteracy, as though if only the patient had learned to read properly, he would never have got into this mess in the first place. By then, government, the universities and industry and commerce were all in rare agreement about management education as the right medicine. As usual the problem wasn't so much in the efficacy of the medicine itself, but the care with which it was administered. The patient still languished. Latterly, the economists, a specialized, quackish arm of the medical metaphor, pronounced advanced malnutrition of investment money, as if all that was needed was a good meal. Unfortunately, the cupboard was already almost bare. By that time also government appeared to have defined *its* primary task as the maintenance of full employment or, at any rate, the maintenance of its appearance. This seemed to some to be tantamount to bringing in the make-up girls in order to cause the patient to *look* healthier.

My own diagnosis would be a severe bout of the vapours – a traditional English description of vague illnesses of depression, spleen and hypochondria at which doctors throw up their hands (provided they are not engaged in writing prescriptions). Ivan Illich coined the phrase 'medical iatrogenesis', that is, the collusive subconscious process through which doctors render their patients sicker than ever, thus ensuring continuity of supply. Structural iatrogenesis he defines as a backlash – 'the paralysis of healthy responses to suffering'. That is no bad description of the British difficulty in mobilizing Fight.

The kinds of collusive relationships to which Illich refers are not uncommon. Just as doctors have a vested interest in sickness, so do priests have a vested interest in sin; so too does every victim require a murderer. The widespread adoption of the medical analogy for British industry is an important phenomenon. The iatrogenic argument states that the extent and seriousness of sickness is a function of the number of doctors, rather than vice-versa. It is a similar phenomenon to Professor Parkinson's observation that the number of admirals in the British navy dictates the fullness of their in-trays, rather than the number of capital ships. I commented in Chapter 5 that nowadays almost everybody leaving school for university wants to be a doctor (or a lawyer). Arguably, the relative unpopularity of engineering has nothing to do with its intrinsic appeal but a great deal to do with its associations with the split-off, hard, industrial sub-culture. Conversely, the appeal of medicine, in a feminine, care-dominated culture, is obvious. The medical analogy is creeping into industry itself as the army and family models in particular begin to become less fashionable. The central problem is to determine how much of the undoubted sickness of industry is intrinsic and how much projected into industry by the legions of experts all around. The picture in my head is of a hospital bed, so surrounded by specialists (many of them quacks) that the patient is gasping for air.

The patient with schizoid tendencies is one whose parts remain split, feeding off and sustaining each other, but essentially unintegrated, incapable of resolution into a whole because of fear of some fantasized destruction. Such a person is, literally, without integrity. The obvious split in Britain is that between ownership and workers represented by the unions – the traditional, familiar, binary split of a class society. Yet, I find it somehow unconvincing precisely because it has taken on so familiar and so symbolic a character. Anyway, I regard the British class system as essentially an art form. Everybody seems to enjoy it; and bosses and workers, but not their multi-tudinous intermediaries (foremen, supervisors, charge-hands, etc.), usually get on fine. It was the late Allan Flanders who observed that, relative to the American pattern, British trade union activity was excessively concerned with *procedure* rather than substance, as though the primary task was to find a structure of *relationships* which would express an underlying perception of the world, rather than to negotiate, or fight, about concrete issues. My tentative guess would be that a deeper, more destructive, and hence more frightening, split is to be found between the assumptions of caring and Dependence in society at large and the assumptions of hardness and Fight which are projected into industry. These underlying assumptions I have symbolized, perhaps over-simply, as feminine and masculine. It is not uncommon in the schizoid patient for the obvious split, presented, as it were, on a plate to the doctor or shrink, to represent a displacement of something deeper and more frightening.

In that context, the emergence in the 1970s of the 'voice' of management in the form of the British Institute of Management (the British equivalent of the American, Australian and Irish Management Institutes, but difficult to relate to Continental bodies) may be of historical significance. As I have outlined, the idea of 'management' has always represented, amongst other things, the hope of integration of the 'two sides' of industry – notably in the 1920s and latterly after World War II. The idea of managers having a 'voice' sounds like fighting talk, but may well express the Dependent state of those in the middle, what one manager of my acquaintance calls the 'mink-lined trap'. In other words, if the owners and the trade unions get to talk to the Prime Minister (at the centre of things), the managers want to be in there too. Those who speak for managers will have to be very canny indeed to avoid being captured by the culture of dependence and drawn into a cosy new club with as little lasting impact as all those structurally identical initiatives that have gone before. To speak for managers today and especially for the junior, the underemployed in Mickey Mouse jobs, the manufacturers in impossible jobs and the growing number of redundants – means taking inside oneself depression, alienation and even chaos and trying to represent that chaos in polite society — like emitting a loud belch at a smart cocktail party.

All this represents a rather (i) complicated, and (ii) tentative analysis of the scene. As such, it can be shot down on the grounds that it is (i) theoretical (the favourite defence of the 'practical' split in British industry) and/or (ii) unscientific (the favourite defence of the notionally clever 'intellectual' split). The idea that processes like psychological projection, familiar in the theory of small groups, may operate on a vast scale is not widely accepted. In fact, very little is known about human behaviour at this level. We are capable of technical achievement of extraordinary virtuosity and intricacy, like picking up a handful of dust on Mars at a range of 36 million miles, but we cannot say for sure why Germany tipped towards

Hitler in the 1930s nor whether or when such things may happen again. Perhaps the most tragic contemporary example of mass splitting is to be found in Northern Ireland not, once again, the old and familiar religious split, nor even the class split, but the subtler division of population into those, even children, who are pumped full of blind hatred to the point of madness and those decent folk on the comfortable outskirts of the troubles, deploring it all but taking no responsibility at all for the projection of their own prejudice and panic into others. There can be little doubt that some of the more spectacular killers in Ulster are not, so to speak, themselves, but receptacles for massive psychological projections of others.

Faced by catastrophe on this scale, it would seem to represent Flight on a grand scale to neglect such theoretical probings on the grounds that they are not 'proven'. We have proof enough about the six million Jews, but we still don't really understand why it happened as it did. I have digressed somewhat from the relatively benign problems of British industrial management in relation to society, but with a purpose. In times past of relative affluence when an accepted fabric of authority structures of many kinds bound society together – the church, the family, the local school, government – the British propensity for split thought represented little more than a relatively harmless eccentricity. But things have changed for the worse. Areas of unremitted poverty have persisted with an increasing sense of social injustice. Historically, poverty and a sense of deep injustice are the harbingers of drastic social and political shifts. Faith in the binding institutions of society has drained away, partly because those institutions themselves have been ill-adapted to change circumstances but *mostly* because we have not learned how to ensure that people of vision and integrity, of whom there is an adequate supply, rise to the top of them. Further, traditional modes of split thinking have taken on more sinister, pathological overtones with respect to, for example, race.

Britain has not yet broken down into a tribal society, but if such splits as exist persist and deepen the risk is always there. Systems theory demonstrates that all systems – social systems, eco-systems etc. have a substantial 'domain of stability' within which substantial environmental changes can be absorbed and adapted to. However, the tip-over point into system break-down can be arrived at suddenly and unpredictably, as events in the Congo and in Ulster have demonstrated. At the emotional level, failed dependence leads to infantilization and primitive survival behaviour. It *has* been a dependency culture, unable, or unwilling to take up the fights that really matter and there is now an acute, shared, sense of failure. It is a situation where the business and industrial sub-culture, for all its frailties, has something of paramount importance to teach society as a whole – that is, something of the long-term view or how to be cruel to be kind. Instead of listening, society at large simply projects its own inadequacies about rigour, competitiveness and toughness into the business sub-culture. It *is* time that the sub-culture spoke out for itself, not in the usual borrowed 'professional' clothing (borrowed from a strikingly corrupt 'professional' sector, unlike anything to be found elsewhere in Europe) but from its own distinctive identity, warts and all. How that may be done is the theme of Chapter 10.

10 Fighting the good fight

I have painted a picture of a split society in a state of Dependence. Furthermore, it is a society which misdirects its Fight into fruitless and clichéd areas of contention, while more important fights lie uncontested. If the country was a patient, the task would be to integrate the parts into a sensible whole in relation to the environment, not without internal conflict, but ensuring that inevitable conflict bore some relation to national purposes. Naturally, I am talking about leadership and the capacity of leaders to grasp that a country is more than a big economic contraption; it has a psychology which, with insight and application can be understood and used as a yardstick for proposed change. Where does one begin the process of integration, of rediscovering integrity? How can the despised wealth creators find their own intrinsic integrity?

Being horrid about the professionals

In Chapter 1, I noted that the 'professional' superstructure to be found in Britain is paralleled nowhere else in Europe. Furthermore, this structure appears to have rather a lot to do with social status and ideology (that is, *being*) and rather too little to do with standards of the output (that is, *doing*). I was careful to refer, above, to the 'professionals' rather than the professions. As they say, France would be a wonderful country if it weren't for the French. What the *professions* have always stood for is very important indeed – that is, self-regulation of standards and the ensurance that clients may be properly identified, contracted with and provided with recourse against incompetence. However, in recent years, the old professions have swung alarmingly away from the Work end of the Work/

Survival continuum into survival type behaviour. The most obvious manifestation is the increasing tendency of professionals to behave like the more unregenerate elements of the trade union movement. It is an understandable shift; pay differentials have been eroded and a growing number of professionals such as doctors and teachers are nowadays simply salaried employees of large bureaucratic organizations. In such circumstances, the client, the *raison d'etre* of the 'professional' structure, begins to merge into the shadows.

But, in a culture of being rather than doing, the industrial managers have remained obsessed with the status rather than the *actions* of the professional classes. In practice, the lawyers (the experts on cartel) have created a cartel of immense proportions; the doctors have helped to create a grossly unnecessary drugs industry and a substantial corpus of more or less neurotic people prepared to define themselves as sick; the architects have colluded with the planners and government officials to construct a sub-culture of sub-standard people in dehumanized and dehumanizing public housing; the 'scientists' have pressed on with their arcane and extravagant enquiries as if 'science' itself was God, and people its proper subjects. Virtually the only profession to emerge from the post-war years with substantially lowered status has been engineering; the one profession in fact where the test of utility is inescapable. Perhaps that is why.

The professions are not without their internal critics, but it can be no easy matter to reverse such tendencies when so many new entrants to the most prestigious 'professional' jobs are there for personal gain and status (what you take out) rather than the intrinsic purposes of the work (what you have to put in). It could be said that the failures of the professions are, in fact, failures of *management* – that is, an inability to adapt to changing environmental circumstances, to manage the boundary region between the profession itself and the new bureaucracies with which most of them now have to deal. I am not, thus, trying to be horrible about the thousands of dedicated doctors, teachers and so on, who have kept faith with their clients and kept their humility as a result.

Instead, I am suggesting that no sensible industrial manager can delude himself for long that he operates in a vacuum. If the management is wrong, he may have to fight to do something about it; otherwise he could end up without a job himself. Because he might, conceivably, get the sack as a result of his or somebody else's, incompetence, his grasp of the concept of accountability has a different, and more immediate, flavour to that of a typical professional, even though accountability, of a sort, is the underpinning of professional organization. The industrial manager has much to teach the professional about *doing*, but he cannot do it if he is obsessed with *being* like a 'professional' and thus obsessed with rejoining the dependent mother-culture. A necessary prelude to rediscovery of his realistic identity may be a timely *fight* back against what amounts, in times of scarcity, to a natural enemy. To requote Rice, it is not a matter of fight being right or wrong, but of asking if this might be a *useful* fight, in the long run.

Reality, integrity and the managerial role

Getting the 'professions' in perspective is an important task, but not so important as getting the industrial manager's role in perspective. Integrity and identity reside in being what you *are* rather than pretending to be something else. Integrity is assured when, having discovered that what you are is insupportable, you fight to change it. Let me give an example. I worked as consultant once to a group of administrative managers in an aggressive sales organization. There was no question here that the sales force occupied top place in the status pecking order and, appropriately it seemed to me, the highest rewards went to those who ran the greatest risks. Like many sales offices, the walls were adorned with competitive barometers of performance – salesman versus salesman, group versus group, district versus district. Here was accountability in a crude and public form – graphic evidence of who was the least successful, second least successful salesman and so on. (It has been observed before that perhaps the most important symbolic role in such a setting is that of the least successful salesman. All the salesmen provide him with a form of encouragement and succour whilst subconsciously ensuring, for obvious reasons, that he continues to fill that crucial role.) Here too were the usual monthly sales contests structured around those flagging products that the factories had over-produced.

My story really concerns the administrators whose job was to provide a stable base for the operation, ensuring the bills got paid, products delivered, telephones answered, enquiries responded to and so on. In short, their job was to stay at home looking after the housework while the salesmen, engineers and many of the managers went out into the environment in search of prey. The day the administration went, as the Americans say, bananas was the day they began, just like the sales operation, to establish all manner of contests for all manner of baubles in relation to administration performance. They did so because their staff felt in some way inferior to the cocks of the roost – the salesmen. Very soon, much of their effective time was devoted to devising quantifiable criteria by which performance could be measured for this purpose. They did their best with this, but when the trinkets began to be distributed as 'morale boosters', the fights began to break out about the injustices arising out of the inevitable inadequacy of the criteria for the measurement of housewifely qualities. Some of the saner members of the system began to ask why such extras needed to be provided for administrators who were simply doing their jobs. It was the right question.

In the end, the problem for the administrators, mostly men, was to accept the realistic housewifely character of their work and to recognize that the provision of a service does not imply a loss of virility. It was a subject they ultimately dealt with with great common sense, given some time to think it through. This anecdote has relevance also for Women's Lib which has been in danger of confusing service with subservience. It is an easy confusion to fall into in a culture where the idea of being 'in service' has such emotive force. Studies of airline systems also demonstrate the same apeing of flying staff (glamorous) by ground staff (less glamorous) to the point of obfuscation of the crucial and distinctive ground staff role. I am arguing simply that you cannot borrow your identity; you have to discover it inside yourself and your work and, having done so, fight for it if need be.

This being the case, one would expect that 'management education', 'management development', 'management consultancy', 'management research' etc. would all have bent their energies to helping managers to discover these truths for themselves and to providing them with some ammunition for the ensuing fights. It hasn't happened that way, for the most part. To start with, most of the providers of these commodities style themselves 'professional' in the first place and are thus wedded to the notion that practitioners are ignorant fellows in need of enlightenment from the storehouse of academic knowledge. Even management research has tended to focus on the rational/logical elements in decision-making process, rather than the irrational/illogical types who actually make, or more often, postpone or avoid, decisions. It takes a special sort of consultant, teacher or researcher (i.e. one with humility) to recognize that the manager, though frequently uncultured, is not stupid; his wisdom is simply in an inchoate, instinctive form. To be of any use to him at all is to get at his cast of thought; to get inside his head to see how he constructs his work and his role in relation to it. Then it may be possible not to *change* him but to provide him with a more helpful framework for re-examining his own experience in order to get at its underlying organizational meaning.

There are a number of ways of doing this. I have mentioned 'Action Learning' and the 'Working Conferences' of R. W. Revans and A. K. Rice respectively. Another interesting approach is called 'organizational role analysis', a method developed by the Grubb Institute of Behavioural Studies, a small research and consultancy group in London, whose thinking on these matters is not yet widely known. ORA makes the assumption that a role is not a cage (a current graffito runs, 'All roles are cages, but some are cagier than others'). Rather, role provides a means by which the individual can *preserve* what personal power he has and to regulate it in relation to his organization. Furthermore, the approach is more closely akin to what senior executives in public and private organizations say about their organizations (than to what the organizational theorists tend to think about them) – namely, that any fool can learn the substantive knowledge element of all but the most technical management jobs, but it is much rarer to find people with courage, leadership, insight, judgement, integrity and other such vital imponderables. Senior managers often talk of these *qualities*, simply because they know they matter. Academics tend to be scared of them because they are too vague, emotive and (worst of all) unquantifiable. This is precisely why many academics lack them.

What happens in a 'role consultation' (the vehicle for ORA) is superficially very simple indeed, like most good ideas. The client/ manager meets with a role consultant on about eight to ten occasions, each time for two hours or so. The client will probably begin by talking about his organization and his problems in it. All the substantive input comes from the client; the theoretical constructs for examination of that input are contributed by the consultant. For example, the consultant is unlikely to take notes; it isn't a data gathering exercise but rather a mutual exploration of ideas. More likely, the consultant will be drawing pictures of the organization (rarely straight-forward hierarchical pyramids) which become more complex and subtle as time passes. A role consultation is quite unlike the classical idea of 'counselling'; it usually feels more like a tightly controlled Fight than a situation of Dependence. It is not therefore about the person directly, but rather a close inspection of the organization from the vantage point of a particular *role*. However it is done, it seems to me that attention to *role* is necessary for change, though not perhaps sufficient. The key issue is, what has the manager got up in his head about his role that governs his behaviour?:

Possibly the main blind spot for the typical manager is the idea that the organization he holds in his head is *the* organization. To quote Bruce Reed of the Grubb Institute, 'No one can see an organization, all anyone can see is other people behaving, each according to his own views of reality.' So perhaps the most important penny to drop in a role consultation is the moment when a manager recognizes that he is not simply describing his company, but his own 'map' of it. Furthermore, the map he has mirrors his own beliefs, assumptions and feelings: in attempting to describe his organization he, in part at least, describes himself. To put it another way, he has the organization inside himself and if he experiences the organization, as many do, as a kind of monster, it is a monstrosity, in part at least, of his own creation. In a way, this is an obvious point, but very difficult to grasp for anyone who believes he 'knows' what the situation is.

For example, many people experience their organizations as power networks (rather than formal authority structures) and, depending on how powerful they themselves feel, are prey to feelings of impotence in relation to 'the system'. Such statements as 'Why don't they . . .' and 'You can't beat the system' and 'Don't stick your neck out', reflect this sense of organizations experienced as a kind of impenetrable jungle. The sensation is real enough – a 'fact' for anyone who feels that way. Senior executives tend to complain, with some justice, that their subordinates lack the capacity to stick their necks out, to behave entrepreneurially, to run even moderate risks; but, senior executives are, relatively, safe. They can 'see' relatively more of the organization. Even if it still seems to them to be a power network, it will not frighten them so much, partly because they are more secure, but mostly because their capacity to predict the behaviour of the system is greater. Their internal 'map' is more accurate and covers more of the territory.

Why do people, left to themselves, make their organizations into monsters and their own roles into organizational ciphers? For one thing, it is, though frightening, a *stable* view of the world. If an individual were to feel that he had some purchase on events, then he would probably feel duty bound to 'do something about the situation' instead of complaining 'Why doesn't *somebody* do something about . . .', and *that* might be a really frightening prospect. In fact, the outcome of a role consultation is likely to be that sort of *grasp* of a situation that allows predictions to be made and that sort of 'courage' that derives from knowledge. If you identify your position on the informal organizational 'map', or at least gauge the error of your own map, you can set out in one direction or another with at least a modicum of confidence. If you can return a fortnight later to a role consultation and verify that there are indeed obstacles where predicted, then the possibility is reinforced that it may, just, be possible to take short cuts, bridge organizational chasms, circumnavigate or overcome power politics and run all manner of risks in order to get a *job* done. (Mant, 1976.)

But, before we presume to 'develop' someone in a managerial role, we must ask the awkward question, why he does not, being sane and sensible, develop himself? What particular image of his world does he cling to that makes strait-laced, cautious conservatism seem to be the right approach? I think Dr Fred Emery, writing of Australians (though they might as well be Americans or Englishmen), is absolutely right to suggest that conservatism and timidity cannot be understood simply in relation to the challenges, difficult as they now are, of managerial work:

'*Why will not managers try to help themselves out of the painful paralysis inflicted on them by turbulence?*' The answer has to be, I think, that there is something out there in the future that they fear will turn out more painful than even their present circumstances; if they fool around with the system. They are in a situation of 'better the devil you know than the one you do not'.
In the mid-sixties I saw it as a fear that was focussed on the work-place. For that reason I thought it was a fear that could be overcome by careful, step-by-step demonstration that there was nothing to fear from democratization of the workplace; that greater mutual benefit, mutual respect and co-operation were the outcomes. I no longer think that the focus of that fear was, or is, just on the work-place. That was my hang-up as a social scientist whose main life's work was on work.

My recent studies strongly suggest that the focus all the time was the fear of what was happening in the society at large. What I now suggest is that from about 1956 our Western societies have been in a cultural revolution. The traditional authority structures in all walks of life have been denigrated. Managers, like everyone else, have been exposed to this in their communities, their churches, their leisure activities and *above all in their relations with their children.* They have also lived with the erosion of the traditional status discriminations. Over the past twenty years these experiences were corroding the confidence of managers much more than I had realized. They were after all very much an integral part of the native-born male Establishment. Their authoritarianism in the workplace gained its justification from the good job they were supposed to be doing in supplying the society at large. The widespread challenges they saw in society – the long hair, scruffy clothes, sexual licence, drugs, dropping-out – could not but make them anxious of the very ground on which their career achievements were based.

If they had any theory about what was happening in those past two decades it was either that there had been too much permissiveness and indulgence of children, women, aboriginals and other inferior beings – or that some evil organization was bringing it about by pushing drugs, ideas and porn on to those innocent inferiors. In holding these theories they were not distinguishable from the academic students of these social changes. We were all at sea, except the prophets 'writing on the subway wall'. Faced with the challenge of creating new participative forms in their own work places and their sectors of industry I think they felt they were being asked to add more fuel to a social conflagration that would consume all that their life's career stood for.

This is, I believe, too much to ask of the ordinary mortal manager.

Emery's analysis reinforces my belief that 'management education' and 'management development' (I allow 'management training' as a purely technical affair) are going to have to deal, as I suggested in Chapter 9, with the whole man, values and all, if anybody is going to be changed or, more correctly, helped to adapt to changing circumstances.

Any approach to managerial learning which goes into depth, at length, seems to me to be more likely to bear fruit than a classroom activity. It all depends on how you interpret the difficulties managers undoubtedly meet. Like Revans,* I doubt very much that most managers need a lot of extra knowledge. What they *do* need is a little more get-up-and-go. The question is, where does *that* come from? I doubt a manager can be energized except through close attention to his existing *role*, not in the formal sense, but in the sense of what actually happens and what the meaning of *that* might be. I am harking back here to the work of Sune Carlson (p. 52) and his discovery of the mythologies surrounding managerial work – i.e., the fantasy that every day is 'atypical'.

*Revans knew the theoretical issues from the start. Let me reproduce a quote from him, contained in my report 'The Experienced Manager' (1970): 'A manager can no more affect the movement of pieces upon the chessboard of his own company without himself being pushed around on it, than a gun can fire a shell without recoiling. And just as every gun, whatever may be its intended target, has its own ballistics of recoil, so has every manager his own characteristic pattern of responses to every decision he takes; and these responses will determine how far he learns from whatever practical experience is still in store for him.'

The role-analysis approach I have described above seems to me to be important because:

1 It assumes the manager to have the wisdom he needs already, though he may choose not to use it, for a variety of reasons. Simply to provide him with sophisticated 'management techniques' is rather like giving an incompetent navigator a more powerful car; he will just arrive at the wrong place sooner.

2 It falls somewhere between in-company programmes (occasionally seen by recipients as brain-washing) and external programmes (usually seen as a reward, or a holiday, or a charge of 'motivation', or a *personal* freak-out). The concept of role, much misused, is the bridge between institutional life (for which part of life salaries are paid) and individual life.

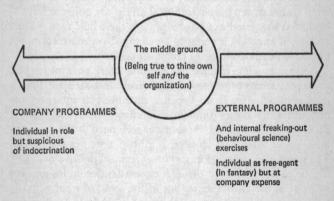

The middle ground

(Being true to thine own self *and* the organization)

COMPANY PROGRAMMES

Individual in role but suspicious of indoctrination

EXTERNAL PROGRAMMES

And internal freaking-out (behavioural science) exercises

Individual as free-agent (in fantasy) but at company expense

3 It recognizes, in the intensity of the work, that no one in his right mind is going to change his behaviour unless he goes through the agony of discarding, and suitably mourning, old and comfy ideas about what he is up to in his work. Learning – the real McCoy, the kind that actually changes people – hurts a bit. We might as well face the fact and set about institutionalizing learning structures of sufficient solidity and purpose to do the job. That shift of emphasis would, I am afraid, render obsolete a great many 'management' teachers.

Education and Development happen to be particular interests of mine, possibly as a result of never quite understanding what on earth my own schooling was about. I have no illusions, however, that the structures and institutions which surround us are far more potent determinants of our behaviour than any kind of education we may receive in adulthood. Nonetheless, I am left worrying about some of the least studied role-incumbents of all – Members of Parliament, Congressmen, members of Cabinets, etc. Who on earth do they turn to for spiritual and intellectual succour – the boss? (at the risk of time-wasting or seeming to be weak) – colleagues? (competitors for resources) – government officials? (at risk of fudging a crucial boundary) – a pal? (certain to be viewed with suspicion and quite without formal authority) – spouse? (at serious risk of the marriage). Management education, as it has developed, goes nowhere near this sort of problem. Some kind of long-term consultation seems to me to be the best prospect, suitably hedged around with all the safeguards of a professional relationship. Holders of the highest offices do not seem to be 'managing' very well and it is, no doubt, time we gave some thought to the problem.

Power and authority

It may be a symptom of our times that for many people 'authority' has become a dirty word, almost a synonym for 'authoritarian', and the word 'power' has effectively replaced it. In this construction, to be subject to authority is to be robbed of power. In fact, the truth is the opposite. The decline of traditional authority structures has robbed many people of any sense of taking up a role in any kind of recognizable and respected institution. This rolelessness leads to a sense of powerlessness and the associated obsession with power. Obsession with power leads, in turn, to the projection of power into powerful, charismatic figures, a further reinforcement of dependence. In the end, we have ultimate authority vested in the Queen, a form of authority without teeth for several centuries and a profound belief in the uses of power. A world of power is a world of Survival and survival behaviour. To quote Matthew Arnold 100 years ago:

We are left with nothing but our systems of checks, and our notion of its being the right and happiness of an Englishman to do as far as possible what he likes, we are in danger of drifting towards anarchy. We have not the notion, so familiar on the Continent and to antiquity, of the *State* – the nation in its collective and corporate character, entrusted with stringent powers for the general advantage, and controlling individual wills in the name of an interest far wider than that of individuals.

In the public mind, 'authority' is associated with the traditional professions. The doctor and lawyer have 'authority' and they have it through the existence of the profession, notionally accountable to society for its members. Industry, trade and commerce are, conversely, thought of as domains of *power* and, accordingly, throw up inflated power figures with great regularity. If, however, one looks at power and authority as ideas about social processes, the truth is often the reverse. The professional sector uses power in a variety of subtle ways as I have noted in Chapters 5 and 10 (above), whereas the affairs of business are commonly more visible and subject to public constraint.

In this sense, power and authority are not like qualities at either end of a continuum. Rather, personal power is the main ingredient of organizational life. The organization has authority and grants authority to the people; the people bring the power in with them and funnel it, if they choose to, through organizational roles. It is as if the 'authority' of a familiar object (for example a table) rested in its structure but its *power* to exist can only be understood in terms of atoms and molecules. People are the molecules of an organization and people have power; more or less of it. How much may, as I have suggested before, be a function of genetic endowment and the impact of the first year or so of life. When people have ideas, they may use their personal power to create an *activity system* to carry the ideas through. If the activity system is big and complex enough it will generate roles to facilitate the process by which people carry forward its task. Roles, in turn, have authority by virtue of their association with the task and ultimately, with the original idea. Those who fill roles do not relinquish personal power but *channel it* through the role structure, in the interests of the task. To that extent they have authority. In excess of that, they wield power.

Authority is then what you are *entitled* to do. Problems sometimes arise when individuals begin to feel that what the authority structure permits people to do with their authority has drifted, inappropriately, from the original idea to which people gave their assent. 'I was only doing as I was told', is *the* grotesque plea of twentieth-century history; a plea from out of the Survival system. Institutions then can be seen as in a constant state of tension between the Survival mode and what, in Chapter 7, I called the Work mode. The Survival mode is an outcome of the natural, closed system life of an institution in which everyone works to secure his own power position. The Work mode represents the *function* of the institution in its environment; probably what it was set up to do; the original idea. As I have suggested above, these organizational tensions are reflected in the people it employs; some of them, with a valency for Survival, who use power to achieve their sectional ends and others, with a valency for Work, who look for authority to do their part in discharging the organization's accountability to its environment.

The opposed clusters are then:

Work — Survival
Role — Person
Authority — Power

Thus, the organization is about work, roles and authority. The individual, according to circumstances and character, may find himself pushed towards the Work mode or, alternatively, in the other direction. It is not easy, surrounded by survival behaviour, to keep one's head down to work.

Role and potency

I hope I may be forgiven for invoking, yet again, a sexual metaphor for discussing the concept of role. I do so because the imagery of managers in relation to organizational life is commonly linked with ideas of impotence, powerlessness and castration, accompanied by fantasies of omnipotence. What managers often lack is any sense of an interposing part between

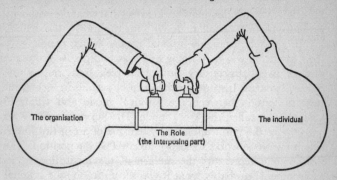

The organisation

The individual

The Role
(the interposing part)

themselves and the organization; they feel, as it were, incorporated whole; swallowed up. I have suggested that role is that interposing part; the seat, as it were, of individual potency in the face of the organization. In *role*, a man may penetrate the organization but, with skill, preserve personal power; injecting only so much as fits the role. As a result he will be experienced by other people *in role*; he can be relied upon to operate according to known, visible assumptions of authority, rather than capriciously, according to personal whim. In short, he can be trusted. Furthermore, if the fit between person and role proves insupportable, he can be clear enough about the issues to withdraw if need be. Without role clarity, he could not be sure; playing the organization along indefinitely, without satisfactory resolution.

I have dwelt on issues of power and authority because most of the managers I meet, and certainly most of those who seem to have problems in coming to terms with their work, have only the vaguest ideas about the difference between power and authority and how it affects them. Middle managers in particular, cut off from any realistic connection with the fundamental, environmental purposes (the idea) of the organization, feel powerless and, accordingly, play power politics. Colin Fletcher has argued, persuasively, that 'management' is finished, that

the current generation of managers cannot survive their employment conditions, that no future generations of managers are being trained

and that the alternatives exercised by managers indicate their
knowledge of these facts. The problem has been with managers all along.
Management is neither art nor science nor skill. At base, there is nothing
to do. A manager is hired for what he knows other firms do; what he can
find to do, and what he can be told to do.

The hero of this piece is the manager; a tragic hero, be-
leaguered on all sides, stripped of identity and, in any other
than Anglo-Saxon culture, a mythical beast. Maybe, as
Fletcher argues, the manager, as opposed to the 'supervisor'
and the 'executive' is doomed, but heroes do not go under
without a struggle. The heroic struggle confronting managers
is to reconnect themselves with organizational purposes – the
idea and thus with the reality of clients. If it can be done, our
hero then has a role (which he can use to regulate and preserve
his personal power) and a sense of identity (properly speaking,
professional identity). That is, in fact, the first step towards
'professionalization' – 'The development of some kind of social
contract between a national community (of clients) and an
occupational group whose effectiveness in meeting important
community needs leads to some kind of contract – some kind
of social sanction and social control, not always by law.'
(A. T. M. Wilson.) The problem facing the manager is that to
reconfront corporate purposes may in some cases present him
with impossibly difficult moral dilemmas. He may, in short,
not much like what he sees at the boundary, to the point where
he must fight to preserve his own integrity. It is not the sort of
fight he is accustomed to getting into.

Education

It is logical to expect 'education' to help people to understand
such matters as power and authority and their importance for
individual and organizational effectiveness. Clearly, it is time
management education recognized that, if the very *raison
d'etre* of 'management' arises out of doubts about legitimacy,
then issues of authority and power must be somewhere near the
top of the educational agenda. But the problem with education
goes further back. Long before a man or woman becomes a

worker, supervisor, manager or executive, he or she will have learned a great deal about power and authority, principally from family and school. At school, it will not have been on the formal curriculum, but it will have been, just the same, an inescapable 'lesson' in the life of the school.

Recently, a mini-scandal erupted over the alleged supression, by the British teachers' union, of a research study which demonstrated that even where the intake of children to a group of schools was near enough identical as to socio-economic background, there were vast differences in the capacity of schools to contain delinquency and get the kids to work. Superficially, it is an unsurprising finding; most of our experience teaches us that the combination of inspired leadership and enthusiastic teamwork can work wonders even in very trying circumstances. Why should teachers' representatives wish to deny such self-evident truths? In this case, it seems the implicit primary task was to assert that the excellence, or otherwise, of a school is a function solely of its pupil intake, or, more succinctly, that teachers cannot be held accountable for grappling with the outputs of deprived communities and families.

No one should underestimate the difficulty of the teacher's job when children, quite sensibly in many cases, can no longer see the point of schooling. But does it really help to deny vagaries of performance as between school and school and teacher and teacher? Is it really in the interests of most teachers to render head teachers unsackable? More to the point, what is likely to be learned, through the skin, by pupils of a system where the authority figures do not feel corporately accountable for what is contained within the system boundary. If the teachers, like the middle managers, find it difficult to establish an authorative role, then the logical outcome is likely to be pupil *power*. The pupil role *has* an implicit authority, but there is no way pupils can discover it in a set-up where the established authority figures have difficulty in distinguishing the difference, in their own behaviour, between power and authority.

Elizabeth Richardson has usefully pointed out how the usual plethora of *ad hoc* committees in the school may be a partly subconscious diversion from the formal authority structure of the staff. If teachers are frightened of authority, or, more correctly, if they have made authority a monster, then there can be little hope that their pupils will be able to find appropriate authority in their own roles. A school which has leaders capable of providing a dependable structure and of managing fight instead of projecting it back into the environment, is a school capable of providing a useful alternative model of institutional life for the many pupils who come from power-dominated homes. Many such schools exist; the tragedy is that we have so little curiosity as to how they came to be that way.

During 1977, Her Majesty's Inspectorate of Schools in the UK published a report entitled 'Ten Good Schools'. As a bit of research, it was refreshingly free of the tortuous irrelevance of most research effort. In short, the Inspectorate decided to take a close look at a diverse group of schools, all of undisputed quality, in order to discover, if possible, how they got that way. Note that the vexed question of defining a 'good school' was neatly sidestepped on the assumption that everybody knows it when they see it. The indices are not difficult to find – pupils actually turn up, teachers fight for jobs there, employers find they can employ the output (and not just as 'cannon-fodder'), the local community takes note of the low level of vandalism, and parents are prepared to move house to get into the appropriate catchment area. The truth is, you can almost smell the quality as soon as you walk in the door of a good school.

The findings of the study are unsurprising. Good schools, it seems, have good head teachers and *they* tend to be tough but fair (my distillation of a long report). That is, they keep their eye on the ball – whenever a teacher deals with the head, the teacher is clear that he or she is not engaged in a personal relationship but an *institutional* one. The head represents, and embodies, the institutional task and is prepared to consult about it and fight for it, if need be. If teachers are able thus to have a *role* relationship with the school, there is at least a chance that pupils can have a role relationship with their teachers. Instead of feeling powerless, pupils may actually become aware of their authority in the role of pupil. It is the best possible way to learn about role, institution, authority and so on, whether such subjects are on the curriculum or not. It is probably the only sure way to learn to take up a responsible role in society.

Ultimately, some of the school pupils go on to university and then, perhaps, to a management school. In all likelihood, their life's experience of education is an experience of real power and elusive authority. To whom is a lecturer accountable and with respect to what? What are the outputs of his activity system and where and how are they applied? What is his *idea* of the role and function of the university in society and how is that reflected in his behaviour? It is no easy matter to find out. Instead, most of the management schools, lacking faith in the intrinsic worth of their products, adopt a 'marketing' approach, as though education were a supermarket commodity. I referred in Chapter 5 to the contrast of Swedish and British visions of 'marketing'; the one straightforward and honest, the other clever but shallow. Here, the schools replicate the worst practices of big business – that is, lack of interest in the integrity of the product itself accompanied by a host of cosmetic changes – a sort of 'badge engineering' – together with vigorous and skilful promotional activity. It is here, unfortunately, that management education is most nearly a mirror-image of 'management'.

Whatever the educational structure – school, university or business school – one can state two simple truths with some confidence:

1 That the throughput of an educational establishment is complex; more, that is, than the students themselves. For example, the secondary school will process incipient delinquency and some will do it much more effectively than others. Teachers have so little grasp of this as a *throughput*, as opposed to a burden, that they are largely unaware that some schools do handle it much better than others, and clueless also about how. Likewise, the business schools have to process the expectations and fantasies of those 'personnel' specialists who have the responsibility for sponsoring individuals for external training. Those fantasies often have little to do with the dominant throughput itself and much to do with

sustaining the prevailing logic of the sponsors' own management structures. The business schools also have to process elements of the 'mid-life crisis', that is, they have to absorb the inevitable depression of those executives who, released perhaps for the first time from manic busyness, begin to *think* about what is happening to their lives. No official statement *says* the mid-life crisis is a throughput; nonetheless, it *is* and will be so long as middle-aged people have to confront the reality of approaching death.

2 That, irrespective of the curriculum, the experience of simply taking up a student role in an educational establishment 'teaches', through the skin, about authority and authority structures. Often, it teaches no more than simple distrust of 'authority' as a vague idea and, thus, a concomitant reliance on personal power for survival. Most teachers would accept this proposition at an intellectual level with very little idea of how their own behaviour may reinforce such prejudices. This cluelessness is summed up in the German joke-professor bellowing, 'You will participate!'

What we have to deal with is that educators are, for the most part, quite naïve about their roles, their institutions' roles and, most of all, the nature of the authority of their students' roles. Most teachers have spent many years learning how to be teachers, most of it content-oriented, even the teaching practice element for those who get it, but know little of the two simple truths above. There are two notable exceptions, to my knowledge. One is to be found in education for the very young, especially those not yet able to read. Here, teachers know that the throughput is complex, even surreal, because the throughput itself has not yet learned to suppress its fantasy life. Here too the sponsoring authority (otherwise known as the mother) has a discernible role and role boundary to be managed. Here, the authority structure derives from the activity system and the activity system is geared to learning by experiencing, exploring, discovering. Teachers often make fools of themselves by misinterpreting the nature of the exploration but, as it is only kids, it tends not to embarrass them too much. I doubt there is much wrong with management education that wouldn't be helped by compulsory assignment of management teachers to the under-fives for, say, a year. Ironically, many management teachers have young children themselves, but never sense the connection between the two throughputs. They have forgotten what it is like to be a child and they have blinded themselves to the reality that the bumptious executive with a company Ford in the car park is made like a child by entering the student role in a strange unfamiliar institution.

I mentioned two exceptions above: the other is a form of education for adults which makes no pretence that entry to education in maturity means anything other than coping with a dependent role. I 'refer here to the 'working conferences' on organization, authority, leadership and power conducted by the Tavistock Institute, and latterly by the Grubb Institute, since 1957. The late A. K. Rice was the principal architect of this extraordinary educational departure – a conference for the study of group and institutional process, with no curriculum, no lectures and none of the familiar sanctions; in many ways, an adult version of the nursery school and rather frightening for all that. All that was provided was a space (say two weeks) and a structure of sub-spaces of one and a half hours (events) for the study (as it happens) of process in different configurations. 'Staff' were supplied to help *interpret* what happened and their authority, along with everything else, was a subject of study as well. The working conference model, as developed by Rice and others, is justly famous and has been replicated by numerous institutions all over the world. It was a startling development in educational theory and practice and the extraordinary thing is how little known it is, even now, in its country of origin, except to a body of afficionados already associated with the attempt to understand subconscious process in the caring professions, personnel, the behavioural side of academia and so on.

As one might expect in the light of history, notable absentees from the learning by experience/working conference world, probably because of its association with intellectualism, reflection and the subconscious, have been those with most to gain from it – the operating managers and trade union officials in business and industry who have to grapple with issues of power and authority in every working moment. Here, once again, is to be found an aspect of Binary Thinking – the splitting of those in the know from those with the need to know. The relative absence of the business people is at least comprehensible – understanding the psychopathology of power politics may be a distressing business if you happen to live in a world of power. But the lack of interest of the academics is more remarkable when one considers that the working conference replicates precisely the underlying psychological structure of a school. If the academics really wanted to understand the *processes* in which they are engaged, tools are available to do so. It is difficult to avoid the conclusion that most teachers prefer not to know. What kind of example is *that* for their pupils?

As I write this, the old, binary argument about technology and education is welling to the surface again in Britain. Should education (the meaningless question goes) turn out 'vocational' cannon-fodder for industry *or* attempt to produce 'well-rounded men'? The educational pendulum is going to swing again and the sadness is that those swinging it (themselves products of the same hopelessly split system) cannot grasp that what has passed for a well-rounded man, for 200 years past, is, as I remarked on p. 117, a bloodless and effete apology for a complete human being – all intellect and no hands or guts. This is, of course, the gist of Hudson's argument (quoted on p. 110) about the splitting of aesthetics from the *making* of things. If education can't help us to be what we *are* – with the wits, the hands and the viscera all connected up – then what on earth is it, save a means of avoiding, for a while, the fights life is made of?

Research

Most of what needs to be said about research has already been said, notably by Liam Hudson, who spelled out the crucial difference between convergent and divergent modes of intelligence. Hudson's insight was that conventional measures of intelligence in fact measure the capacity to converge on a 'right' solution to a limited kind of question. If, however, you put a converger with, say, an I Q of 140, to work on an unusual uses test (how many uses can you think of, for example, for a housebrick?) he is likely to dry up after about six options. The diverger (same IQ) will go on thinking of uses (for example, tombstone for a mouse) until the need for food and rest drives him away. Conventionally, they have the same IQ, yet their modes of thought are clearly quite different.

The nub of Hudson's argument is that the personality and hence the thinking apparatus of convergers and divergers gel at different stages of their lives, for a variety of reasons.

Among convergers, the control of emotional expression is not a matter of personal choice, or conscious decision, but a pervasive feature of their mental life. Where divergers are more open to the irrational elements in their own mental functioning, convergers tend intuitively, automatically, to block these elements out. In a word, they repress them. If late infancy and early childhood are seen as the period during which the child starts to stake out his sense of who he is – to delineate the character he will in future present to himself, and to the world at large . . . convergers can be envisaged as children who construct robust 'ego-boundaries', and include within them only what is rational. Divergers, in contrast, form relatively weak ego-boundaries and allow their own irrational impulses to suffuse their perception of who they are.

The identity of convergent and divergent children can be seen, in other words, as crystallizing to differing extents and at different stages: the convergent during the latency period (i.e. five to thirteen years of age), the divergent in adolescence. The internal economy of the convergent child, the future scientist, might be said to gel at the stage in his development when issues of rationality and internal control are paramount. That of the divergent child, the future arts specialist, sets less firmly, and at a stage when emotional considerations are again more pressing. The convergent child fixates early, on the only constellation of values then available; the divergent child delays, homing eventually on the second constellation of values, the artistic one, which is antithetic to the first.

From such a simple model, a number of predictions flow. If a child fixates early, one would expect him to choose work that is impersonal; to show a limited capacity for introspection and emotional response to people; to be conventional; to be dissociated in his expression of sexuality; to separate clearly his working life from his private life; and to work harmoniously in groups. In contrast, one would expect the child who fixates relatively late to choose work involving people; to show greater capacity for introspection and emotional response; to have relatively little reliance on social conventions; to show a freer, and more integrated, pattern of sexuality; to separate his private life from his work relatively little; and to have difficulty in working in groups. One could also go on to win from the model some of the more apparently paradoxical aspects of the differences between the arts and the sciences. The longer the delay in fixation, the greater the distance – both in time and psychically – between the establishment of a socially presentable self and the untrammelled expression of impulse that characterizes infancy. Hence one would expect what one often seems to find: that the converger, though conventional, is more capable than the diverger of authentic emotional response. In contrast, the late fixator, the diverger, will tend to have recreated his impulsive life in intellectual terms, and to respond, especially in crises, in ways that are at once florid and hollow. One would also expect that the divergent child, being less clearly formed, would experience more turbulence in adolescence than the converger; and that he would be more likely than the converger to throw himself into social life in a disruptive way, pursuing his autobiography at his institution's expense.

Hudson's work is of enormous importance for the art *or* science of management generally and for management research in particular. In the first place, because it may help us to understand the cast of mind of those we call 'managers' and secondly, because it may throw light also on those who purport to apply convergent analyses (research) to essentially divergent activities (running things, to use my own synonym for management). Could one, for example, examine methodically the thinking processes of those in the main functional groupings in the commercial firm – the accountants versus the manufacturers versus the salesmen? Might one find some correlation with the career orientations (Chapter 7) identified by Rapoport? – or the differential ideological turmoil of industrial prime movers noted by Egan? – or my own, rather speculative, ascription of feminine skills to the process of manufacturing? The answer to such questions is probably 'yes', but the answer to the question 'Might you get research funding to pursue them?' is probably 'no'. Yet these are precisely the issues which touch on the *identity* of the manager – which help him to recognize who he is, how he thinks, what he might become.

If my hunch about the binary split of British society into feminine (national) and masculine (sectional) segments has any weight, then one would expect industry and commerce to be clogged up with convergers and the other 'artistic' side to be starved of the *useful* fruits of convergence almost completely. Certainly, Hudson's description of the convergent pattern – impersonality, limited introspection and emotional response to people, conventionality, dissociation in sexual expression, splitting of work and private life and the capacity to work in groups – fits the archetypal executive like a glove. In fact, it matches very closely Maccoby's (Chapter 5) description of 'game character' – the classic, win/lose corporate fighting cock. Furthermore, the 'good company man' can be relied upon *not* to 'pursue his autobiography at his institution's expense' – the mark of the diverger. Where then would the researchers fit in – convergers or divergers?

Notionally, researchers are divergers. After all, research is a way of finding out what you didn't know before. If you can specify in advance that which is going to be discovered then, to a substantial extent, you knew it in the first place. Yet this is precisely the requirement placed upon much management research by the, presumably convergent, officials responsible for the disbursement of funds. The point is that the research approaches which *survive* and thus provide income for their proponents, are those which commerce and industry are prepared to accept. The big bogey for management research is not relevance, but *access* – will they let us in and will we let them in? I have sat on the industry side of that particular fence, listening to the arguments of gormless, youthful academicians as to why their PhD thesis *ought* to be injected into the delicate political network or the firm. They can convince no one. There is no one in their own world to tell them how to do it and only a madman would let them anywhere near the action in order to learn. If it is true that convergent modes of thinking are split-off into the industrial sub-culture, then most of the research is bound, in the end, to be convergent, along with most of the researchers.

Some of the researchers I have applauded – Hudson and

Bion, Egan and Rapoport – are quite unlike each other – in fact these four make rather an odd quartet and I shall not, probably, be thanked by any of them for this enforced company. What they all demonstrate, in their different ways and different fields, is a preparedness to set out into the unknown and a profound respect for and curiosity about their subjects – i.e. people. Working managers in my experience are fascinated by this sort of work; not surprisingly, as it touches so closely on their own, submerged, identities. Yet, such thinkers are rarely to be found on the management education and development menu. Instead, one finds a turgid stream of first- and second-generation American convergers whose ideas have the solitary virtue that they can be grasped and accepted by the 'personnel' people. Managers on courses put up with it because it is nicer, anyway, to be in a country house in agreeable company listening to such anodyne convergent nonsense than grappling with the infuriating divergencies of the line job.

When I draw attention to the divergencies between managers at work and those who 'research' them, I am usually taken to be making an *anti-intellectual* argument for 'relevance', 'applied research' or something of the kind, thus adulterating, it is supposed, academic standards. Not a bit of it; many of the senior executives I know are *cleverer* than top academics, but cleverer in a divergent mode – less bound to little boxes of organized thought and more inclined to take from the Academy whatever seems to fit the moment. But executives frequently *believe* themselves to be somehow dumber than their academic contemporaries and, more heinous still, the academics sometimes confuse learning with wisdom. However, the academics *are* smarter in one way – they have got themselves a much safer, easier and more agreeable occupation.

The best research always seems to be to have a dangerous, divergent air about it, or why bother with research? I have referred before to the Glacier work. This is an account of real events in time and space, over a generation. The ground-rules have changed many times during that period and the numbers of variables to contend with have been awe-inspiring – a nightmare for the kind of researcher who has come to believe that the controlled environment of a laboratory is a boiled-down slice of real life.

Businessmen have not been very good, on the whole, at recognizing kindred spirits in the research trade – that is, those academics, like Elliot Jaques, prepared to grapple with ambiguity and to persevere with something that seems to be important over a long period. But many businessmen have been brainwashed into believing that only what researchers do is truly 'research'. In fact, any effective executive is engaged in unremitting 'research', though in different modes and cycles simultaneously; and that is true for most people, most of the time.

Conclusion

On all these weighty matters, I have no conclusion or recommendations to offer, beyond what is abundantly clear to close observers of the scene already. A great deal of what wants doing in this naughty world seems to be reasonably obvious to men and women of goodwill and common sense everywhere. But we have not, it seems, mastered the trick of creating the intervening institutions that help us to get things done. We have instead a fantasy of freedom and a distrust of institutional restraint and 'red tape' which ultimately binds us. We rush headlong from analysis to action, without stopping en route to build sound constitutional structures to support our endeavours.

It is hard to say whether a distaste for structure is cause or effect of Dependent assumptions in society. Where the rules are fuzzy or non-existent, you must always be in a Dependent state, relying on personal influence and power politics. It is what Erich Fromm has coined the 'escape from freedom'. Paradoxically, it is only in proper structures that proper Fight is possible, otherwise, as managers say, there is going to be 'blood on the ceiling'. In fact, the *threat* of 'blood on the ceiling' causes managers to duck fights; causes them to appear timid when the chips are down. A ducked fight is usually a displaced fight – the blood will be spilled all right, but somewhere else. The fight may even emerge in the form of what the British quaintly describe as 'industrial action'.

We do not, it seems to me, require one penny more spent on fundamental research into the 'unknown', but to understand why we are so bad at putting to use what we know already. I think it quite likely that Britain will show the way forward, not by breaking new ground, but by ploughing old furrows. There is a deeply-embedded constitutional sense in Britain and an instinct for boundaries, both personal and institutional, that is certain to prove useful in a turbulent, overcrowded future.

There is the small matter that British industry and commerce and not a few public bureaucracies appear methodically to have forgotten most of what has been learned over a few hundred years about the importance of 'tough but fair' leadership, and structures which clarify roles and allow people to have a say in things. With luck, this will prove to be an historical aberration; British managers have not exactly forgotten such things, they remember them well enough wearing other hats – as parent, citizen, chairman of the PTA, or in the local pub (a serious and hallowed institution). It is not therefore a matter of learning but of *recollecting* or, at least, discarding some strange Drake-like notions about the world of affairs and work.

But, it is clear, I am as worried as the next man about Britain. Any system, a country or a human being, dependent on others, incapable of Fight about the really important things and essentially wasteful in its enterprises, is in for trouble unless it happens to be very rich. It is not simply a matter of economics either; doing anything less than well is spiritually destroying. Anyway, it is of little use for (say) a destitute family to argue that, in twenty years, all the other families will be the same; the pressing problem is how to survive those intervening years without going crazy.

This book is by way of a salvo from despised 'industry' into the culture at large. We all need, whatever our leanings or our roles, to be 'tough but fair' in everything we do. In a split culture of Dependence, the choice appears to be *Tough* (downmarket) *or Fair* (gentlemanly). If industrial management could take back into itself some of the intellectual subtlety, wit and compassion of the wider culture, it might then be possible for the men of action to re-export to national leaders and others some of the Fight they so often lack.

Britain is the country to watch. If she, with all that accumulated wisdom, cannot find a dignified way to post-industrial society, the odds must lengthen for any of the other developed countries doing so, when the crunch comes.

Bibliography

Preface
Hudson, Liam, 'The Cult of the Fact' (Jonathan Cape, 1972)

Chapter 1
Bendix, Reinhard, *Work and Authority in Industry* (University of California Press, 1974)
Child, J., *British Management Thought* (Allen and Unwin, 1969)
Fores, Michael and Lawrence, Peter, 'What Is Industry' (*New Society*, October, 1978)
Fores, Michael and Rey, L., 'Technik – The Relevance of a Missing Concept' (*Higher Education Review*, London, Spring 1979)
Hudson, L. and Jacot, B., 'Education and Eminence in British Medicine' (*British Medical Journal*, 4, 162, 1971)
Williams, Raymond, *Keywords* (Fontana, 1976)

Chapter 2
Barnett, C., *The Human Factor in British Industrial Decline* (pamphlet: Working Together Campaign, 1975)
Carlson, Sune, *Executive Behaviour* (Stromsbergs, Stockholm, 1951)
Fores, Michael and Glover, Ian, 'The Real Work of Executives' (*Management Today*, November 1976)
Heller, Joseph, *Catch 22* (Corgi, 1972)
Hobsbawm, E. J., *Industry and Empire – 1750 to the Present Day* (Penguin, 1969)
Jaques, Elliott, *A General Theory of Bureaucracy* (Heinemann/Halsted Press, 1976)
Mant, A. D., 'The Manager as Professional' (*Management Today*, September 1975)
Williams, Raymond, *The Long Revolution* (Pelican, 1971)

Chapter 3
Ackoff, R. L., 'A Black Ghetto's Research on a University' (*Operations Research*, Vol. 18, No. 5, 1970)

Bion, Wilfred, *Experiences in Groups* (Tavistock, 1961)

Brown, Lord Wilfred, 'Proposals for Improving the Means of Keeping the Performance of Chief Executives of Companies Under More Effective Scrutiny and Thus Enhancing the Performance of Companies (pamphlet)

Brown, Wilfred and Jaques, Elliott, *Glacier Project Papers* (Heinemann Educational Books, 1965)

Dahrendorf, Ralf, 'Not by Bread Alone' (*Financial Times*, 30 December, 1976)

Mant, Alistair, 'Authority and Task in Manufacturing Operations of Multinational Firms' in *Manufacturing and Management'* (Her Majesty's Stationery Office, London, 1978)

Morris, J. F. and Burgoyne, J. *Developing Resourceful Managers* (IPM, 1973)

Nossiter, Bernard D., *Britain – A Future That Works* (Andre Deutsch, 1978)

Chapter 4

Biendenkopf Report (1970 Report of the Codetermination Commission: Federal Republic of Germany; published by Legal Research Committee, Faculty of Law, Queens University of Belfast, 1976)

Brown, Lord Wilfred, *Exploration in Management* (Pelican, 1965)

Burnham, James, *The Managerial Revolution* (Indiana U.P., 1960)

Chapter 5

Brown, Wilfred, *Organization* (Heinemann Educational Books, 1971)

Fores, M. and Clark, D., 'Why Sweden Manages Better' (*Management Today*, February 1975)

Gorb, Peter, 'How to Manage by Design' (*Management Today*, May 1976)

Hope, Michael, 'On Being Taken Over by Slater-Walker' (*The Journal of Industrial Economics*, Vol. 24, March 1976)

Hudson, Liam, 'Making Things' (*Crafts* Magazine, May/June 1977)

Lawrence, Peter, 'The West German Engineer and the Status of Industry' (*CBI Review*, London, Summer 1977)

Maccoby, Michael, *The Gamesman* (Secker and Warburg, 1977)

Chapter 6

Bower, Marvin, *The Development of Executive Leadership* (Harvard Univ Press)

Drucker, Peter, *The Practice of Management* (Harper and Row, USA, 1954; Pan Books)

Hooher, M. J., *The Development of Executive Talents* (Univ of Michigan Press)

Mace, Myles, *The Growth and Development of the Executive* (Harvard Univ Press)

Mant, A. D. *et al.*, 'Towards Managerial Development for Tomorrow' (unpublished research report for Training Services Agency of UK, 1975)

Planty and Freeston, *Developing Management Ability* (Ranald Press, New York)

Riegal, John, *Executive Development* (Harvard Univ Press)

Chapter 7

Egan, D. and Barron, 'Leaders and Innovators in Irish Industry' (*Journal of Management Studies*, 1968)

Erikson, Erik, *Identity – Youth and Crisis* (Faber, 1958)

Jaques, Elliott, *Work, Creativity and Social Justice* (Heinemann, 1970)

Menzies, I. E. P., *The Functioning of Social Systems as a Defence Against Anxiety* (Tavistock Pamphlet No. 3, reprinted 1968)

Palmer, B. W. M., 'Thinking about Thought' (*Human Relations*, Vol. 26, No. 1, 1973)

Palmer, B. W. M. and Reed, B. D., *An Introduction to Organizational Behaviour* (The Grubb Institute of Behavioural Studies, London 1972)

Rapoport, R. N., *Mid-Career Development* (Tavistock, 1970)

Chapter 8

Franks, Lord Oliver, *British Business Schools* (report, 1963)

Mant, Alistair, *An Open-Systems Model of Business School Activity* (Social Science Research Council, final report, 1975)

Revans, R. W., *Developing Effective Managers* (Praeger, 1971)

Rice, A. K., *Learning For Leadership* (Tavistock, 1965)

Rice, A. K., *Productivity and Social Organization – The Ahmedabad Experiment* (Tavistock, 1958)

Chapter 9

Illich, Ivan, *Medical Nemesis* (Calder and Boyars, 1975)

Chapter 10

Arnold, Matthew, *Culture and Anarchy* (1869)

Dept of Education and Science, *Ten Good Schools: A Secondary School Enquiry* (Her Majesty's Stationery Office, London, 1977)

Emery, F., 'The Ennui of Management' (*National Labour Institute Bulletin*, New Delhi, Jan 1978)

Fletcher, C., 'The End of Management' in *Man and Organization* ed. Child, J. (Allen and Unwin, 1973)

Hudson, Liam, *op. cit.*

Mant, Alistair, 'How to Analyse Management' (*Management Today*, October 1976)

Mant, Alistair, *The Experienced Manager* (BIM Publications, January 1970)

Miller, E. J. and Rice, A. K., *Systems of Organization* (Tavistock, 1967)

Reed, B. D., 'Organizational Role Analysis' in *Developing Social Skills in Managers* ed. C. L. Cooper (ATM, 1976)

Richardson, Elizabeth, *The Teacher, The School and the Task of Management* (Heinemann, 1973)

Wilson, A. T. M., in *Concluding Notes of European Foundation for Management Development Conference* (Berlin, 1976)

Index

Accountants 97–8
Ackoff, Russell 72, 73, 162
Action-learning 74, 164, 171
'All-Round Man' 45, 116–17, 201
America
  German element in 23, 75–6
  management compared with
    Britain 40, 48, 49, 93, 97
  management theorists in 21–2,
    23, 127
  relationship with Britain 75–85
Americans 43, 46, 61, 63, 71
Anglo-USA Productivity Study
  Team 122
Arnold, Matthew qu. 191
Arnold, Dr Thomas 45
Australia, management in 24—5
Authority 73, 79, 191–3, 196–7,
  199
  source of 9, 96, 117, 162
Authority structure 118

Barnett, C. 39, 42, 44
Basic assumption behaviour 62,
  65, 68, 71, 72; see also Dependence, Fight, Survival
Bell System Company study 139
Bendix, Reinhard 22
Binary thinking 18, 26, 36, 41,
  45, 46, 48–9, 64, 81, 96, 111,
  115, 159, 173, 200–201
Bion, Dr W. R. 9, 61–2, 65, 72,
  147, 156, 205

Board of directors 66, 67, 68
Bread manufacture 101–2
Britain, industrial decline in
  39–47, 105, 128, 172, 174
British Institute of Management
  16, 93, 178
Brown, Lord Wilfred 9, 68, 73,
  88, 89
Burgoyne, J. qu. 79
Burnham, James 86, 87, 128

Career development 29, 131,
  140, 145, 155, 168
Carlson, Sune 52, 53, 189
Chief executives 67–8, 124, 158
Child, John 26, 50, qu. 55, 56
Cobden, Richard 40
Computer industry 82
Constitutionalism 87–91, 119
Control 32, 86
Convergers/divergers 145–6,
  201–3, 204–5
Coronary heart disease 139–40
Crittall-Hope company 117–18
Crosland, Anthony 87

Dahrendorf, Ralf 69
Decision making 25, 49, 52–3,
  58, 164, 168
Dependence behaviour 33, 54, 56,
  59–85, 91, 94, 105–6, 113, 146,
  156, 174, 177, 207
Development and training 127

Drake, Sir Francis 31–6, 37, 43, 62, 89
Drucker, Peter 127–8

Educational system 29, 40, 44, 45–6, 58, 80, 159
continental 58, 159
Egan and Barron 142, 146, 203, 205
Emery, Dr Fred 188, 189
Emotional patterns 62, 65
see Basic assumption behaviour
Employees, rights of 60, 88
Engineering profession 58, 106, 177, 182
Entrepreneurship 31–2, 35, 37, 44, 54, 147
Erikson, Erik 136, 137
Executive development 127

Family, as behaviour model 69, 130, 134, 151, 155
Fight, Fight/Flight behaviour 33, 56, 61–76 passim, 85, 94, 97, 113, 146, 174, 177
Flanders, Allan 177
Fletcher, Colin 194–5
Fores, M. qu. 18, 27
France, French 40, 42, 43, 58, 70
Friedman, Milton 172, 173
Fromm, Erich 207

Galbraith, J. K. 37, 147
General Strike 1926 54
Generalist/specialist concept 96, 103, 109
Generativity 137
George, C. S. Jnr qu. 22
Germany, Germans 40, 43, 46, 50, 58, 61, 63, 69, 76
management in 16, 42, 67, 91, 106, 174

Glacier Project (Glacier Metal Company) 73, 88–91, 205
Greed 43, 44 98
Grubb Institute of Behavioural Studies 9, 185, 200

Hall, Noel 80
Harvard Business School 77, 159
Heller, Joseph 54
Henley Administration Staff College 80, 145, 159,
Herzberg, Professor F. 76
Hobsbawn, E. J. 39, 40, 46
Honesty 34–5, 144
Hope, Michael 117
Hudson Institute 42, 70, 204
Hudson, Liam 7, 19, qu. 110, 111, 201–3, 204
Human relations 54–5, 56, 81, 112
'Human stock control' 126–33

Illich, Ivan 65, qu. 71, 176
Industrial Administration, Institute of 51
Industrial democracy 50, 174
Industrial development 127
Industrial Man 117
Industrial relations 28, 157, 175
Industrial Revolution 26–7, 29, 43
Industrial training 127
Industrial welfare 47, 59, 64
Industrialization 43–4
Integrity 101, 109, 157, 181, 183
Ireland 142, 143, 144

Japan, Japanese 59, 61, 63, 90
Jaques, Dr Elliot 73, 88, 136, 138, 206

Labour relations 54, 113
Lawrence, Peter qu. 27

Leadership 22, 53, 54, 56, 78–9
   80, 107, 157, 168, 171, 208
Linguistics 15–30
London Business School 160, 161,
   162
London, City of 34
Loyalty 59, 79
Luck 142, 143, 146
Lupton, Professor Tom 143

MacCoby, Michael 96–7
Man-management 33
Management
   American concept of 22–4, 40
   definitions 11–14, 30, 53, 168
   derivation of term 20
   product of culture 15, 158
   profession of 16, 19, 23, 42
   scientific 51–4
   tasks of 56–7, 91, 119, 178
'Management by Objectives' 157
Management consultancy 76–7,
   81, 185
Management development 57,
   73–4, 77, 84–5, 121–33, 134–58,
   189
   failures of 157–8, 185
   models 129–31, 134, 151, 155
   social defence system 148–51
Management education 16, 57,
   58, 73, 75, 77, 84, 128, 136, 155,
   159–71, 176, 185, 189, 195,
   198
Management movement 49, 51,
   129
Management science 52
Management schools 198–9
Manager
   as agent of owners 21, 37–47, 50,
      56
   as middleman 48–51, 56
   as scapegoat 91–4

   as 'scientist' 51–3, 56
   as technocrat 86–8
   buccaneer prototype 31–5
   evolution of 37, 55–6, 87
   functions of 13, 14, 26, 30
   human relations and 53–5, 56
   identification of 16
   management education and 161
   qualities of 63, 79, 120, 161, 186
   role of 185, 189, 195
Manchester Business School 103,
   160
Mantua Project, Philadelphia
   72–3
Manufacturing 18, 19
Marketing 12, 100, 113, 198
Marshall Aid 76
Massachusetts Institute of
   Technology 159
Mayo, Elton 55
Medical profession 19, 65, 182
Mercedes Benz 101
Mid-life crisis 135–6, 137, 138,
   199
Middle management 37, 38–9,
   107, 168, 194
Military model of management
   53, 78–81, 129–30, 134, 155
Miller, Dr Eric 9
Morris, Professor John F. 9, 72,
   qu. 79, 103
Motivation, management by 55,
   58, 76

North Sea Oil 71
Northern Ireland 179
Nossiter, Bernard 59, 71, 172–3

Organizational Role Analysis 171,
   185, 186–90
Organizational structure 53, 67
Owen, Robert 21 173, 174

Pairing 62, 72, 73, 74
Patronage 134
Platt Clothiers Ltd 107–9
Power 191–2
Power networks 118, 143, 151, 187
Product integrity 101
Product management 95–120, 162
Professionalism 51, 52, 56, 57–8, 87–8
Professions 57, 65, 114, 176–7, 181, 192

Quakers, Quaker companies 47–8, 50, 55, 89, 144

Rapoport, Dr Robert 145, 146, 203, 205
Reed, Bruce 9, 56, 171, 186
Research 201–6
Revans, Professor R. W. 9, 73, 74, 162, 163–4, 171, 185, 189
Rice, Dr A. K. 9, 74, 162, 163–4, 174, 183, 185, 200
Richardson, Elizabeth 196
Riegal, John *qu.* 127
Robens, Lord 172, 173
Roles 185–91, 192, 194
Rolls-Royce 111

Salesmen, selling 12, 13, 100, 113–14, 153, 183–4
Schools 29, 130–31, 134, 155, 196–8
Science, pure and applied 17, 18, 46
Shop stewards 107

Slater-Walker 117–18
Standards, maintenance of 83–4, 107
State ownership 86
Steel production 41, 42
Stewardship 50
Stock Exchange outlook 117
Success 135–6, 142, 144–8
Survival behaviour 39, 56, 138, 139, 147, 152–7, 168, 182, 191, 193
Sweden, Swedes 27, 28, 42, 43, 58, 69, 83–4, 96, 100, 106, 132

Tavistock Institute, London 9, 88, 163, 200
Taylor, theorist 22
'Them and Us' 38, 85, 174
Training Within Industry 75
Trusteeship 56–7, 137, 168

Unions 25, 50, 54, 55, 66, 174, 177
United States *see* America
Universities 74, 77, 106–7, 131
Urwick, Colonel 53, 80

Waugh, Evelyn 95
Weinstock, Sir Arnold 73
Williams, Raymond 21, 43, 46
Wilson, A. T. M. *qu.* 195
Women in industry 111–16, 148, 150
Work Survival continuum 137–8, 139, 152–4, 156, 181–2, 193
Working conferences 163, 200
Wrice, Herman 72, 73